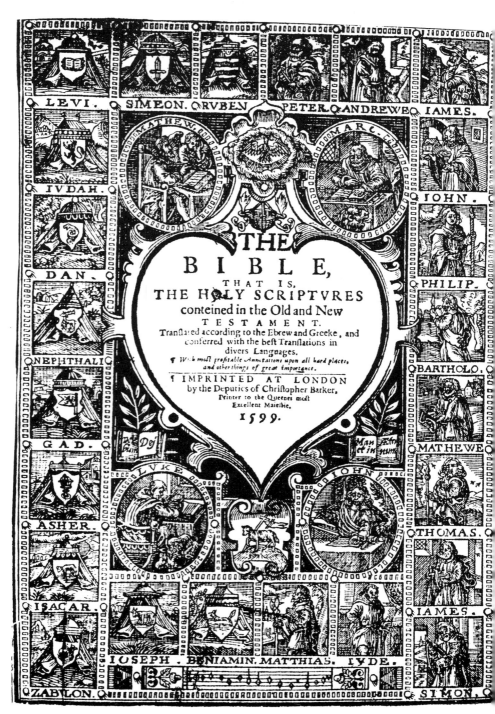

1: Title page of the 'Barker' Bible (1599)

Some Royal Arch Terms Examined

Roy A. Wells, PAGSoj

ENLARGED SECOND EDITION

LONDON

LEWIS MASONIC

© Roy A. Wells
First published in England 1978
This edition revised and enlarged 1988
ISBN 0 85318 154 3

Published by
LEWIS MASONIC, IAN ALLAN REGALIA LTD
Terminal House, Shepperton, TW17 8AS
who are members of the IAN ALLAN GROUP

Previous titles by the same author
Royal Arch Matters
The Rise and Development of Organised Freemasonry
Freemasonry in London from 1785

British Library Cataloguing in Publication Data

Wells, Roy A.
  Some Royal Arch terms examined.
  Enlarged 2nd Edn
  1. Freemasons—Terminology
  I. Title
  366'.1'014   HS395

  ISBN 0–85318–154–3

Printed and bound in Great Britain by
Latimer Trend & Company Ltd, Plymouth

CONTENTS

LIST OF ILLUSTRATIONS

PREFACE TO SECOND EDITION

Some Royal Arch Terms Examined was first published in 1978 and it was thought at that time it would appeal only to a specialised readership. However, after a few years it was virtually unobtainable and requests for a reprint were made from various parts of the masonic world. In this enlarged second edition the author has taken the opportunity to cater for several points that have arisen since then. For those who do not have easy access to the *Transactions* of Quatuor Coronati Lodge, the author's original study of Names given to the Triangle (under the heading of *The Royal Arch Word which signifies 'Soul of Nature'*, *AQC* Vol. 77, 1964) has now been included. Also, a chapter on The Triple Tau, an entirely new work, as well as an extensive list of common pronunciations to meet many requests. In that field, the author stresses that even with purist Hebraists, pronunciation may well vary between Askenasi and Sephardi, even from synagogue to synagogue within one sect, just as the sound of a word may change in churches in England from county to county owing to local dialect. It is emphasised that the list herein is but a guide to common pronunciation of the *Anglicised form* of a *non-English word* in order that it may become recognisable to a reader of that word. Among a given number of Companions in the Order there is likely to be an equal number of opinions and choice, but where personal preference exists, then so be it; nothing should be classed as 'wrong', just 'different', and condemnation should be left to the pedant. This list may help to avoid that sharp intake of breath when a Companion is heard to struggle with an unfamiliar word; for there is always someone, somewhere, who will be ready to make his challenge, but surely that is something we have all learned to live with and accept in Freemasonry.

R.A.W.

AN EXPLANATION OF THE FRONTISPIECE

The title page of the Christopher Barker Bible, dated 1599, shown as the frontispiece, has an arrangement with several points of Royal Arch interest showing a balance between the Old and New Testaments of the bible.

Appearing on the left half of the plate are names and 'banners' of the twelve tribes of Israel, and it should be noted that both Joseph's name and that of Levi appear. Because the tribe of Levi were assigned to priestly duties, responsible for the transportation of the Ark of the Covenant and held in the centre of all twelve whilst in the wilderness of Sinai, the banner does not appear in the Royal Arch but the name often linked with that of Simeon. In the Royal Arch, the places that would otherwise be taken by Joseph and Levi, the names and banners of the powerful and leading tribes of Mannasseh and Ephraim are shown, being the sons of Joseph and at his request received the blessings of their grandfather Jacob.

As a countermatch to the twelve tribes of Israel, the names and representative pictures of the twelve Apostles are shown on the right half of the plate. At the four corners of the central panel the four Evangelists are shown, Matthew, Mark, Luke, and John, each with their representative symbol, i.e., an Angel (Man) for Matthew, Lion for Mark, an Ox for Luke, and an eagle for John.

In the centre, above the actual title, is shown a Dove, emblematical of the Holy Spirit. At the centre, below the title, the Paschal Lamb, *Agnus Dei* or Lamb of God symbolising He who was to be sacrificed as a redemption for mankind. He who was prepared for his ministry on earth by John the Baptist who is described in early masonic catechisms in general:

> He being the forerunner of our Saviour, preached repentance in the Wilderness, and drew the first line of the Gospel.

That reference provides an explanation for the diagram of the circle between two lines, often depicted in masonic drawings and featured in many Tracing Boards for the First Degree. One line is representative of

John the Baptist and the other for St. John the Evangelist of whom the same catechisms state:

who finished by his learning what the other had begun by his zeal.

The circle between the lines symbolises the ministry on earth of Jesus Christ, and the point in the centre of the circle the positioning of the Compasses by the Almighty Architect of the Universe, so well depicted in William Blake's inspired engraving *The Ancient of Days*. The 'Point within a Circle' being thus symbolical of the Almighty Architect.

2:   'The Ancient of Days'
(William Blake)

INTRODUCTION

MANY of the terms brought into Freemasonry, especially in the Royal Arch, have combined to make a biblical exercise of considerable interest and it is from that standpoint the present examination has been conducted.

The importance of the Bible in Freemasony is emphasised in the statement, *Aims and Relationships of the Craft*, issued jointly in August 1938 by the Grand Lodges of England, Ireland, and Scotland:

> 'The Bible, referred to by Freemasons as the Volume of the Sacred Law, is always open in Lodges. Every candidate is required to take his Obligation on that book or on the Volume which is held by his particular creed to impart sanctity to an oath or promise taken upon it.'

This 'Forme of giveing the Mason Word' as it was termed in the *Edinburgh Register House MS* (1696) has its basis in the practice described in early Rolls and MSS of which the following extracts are excellent examples:

> 'THESE CHARGES THAT WEE HAVE now rehearsed unto yow all and all others that belong to Masons yee shall keepe, so healpe you god and your hallydome, and by this booke in yor hande unto yor power.   AMEN, SOBEIT.'
> (*Grand Lodge MS, No.* 1, 1583)

> 'Heare followeth the worthy and godly Oath of Masones. One of the eldest taking the Bible shall hould it forth that hee or the [they] which are to bee maid Masones, may Impoase and lay thear Right hand upon it and then the Charge shall bee read.'
> (*Colne MS. No.* 1, c. 1685)

In that small ceremonial the Bible was used in conjunction with the reading of the *Old Charges*, but before the appearance of the printed Bible, or even its later availability, as the quantity of hand printed copies from 1535 onwards must have been somewhat limited, the scrolls must have served their solemn purpose. They contained charges on behaviour, the observance of Laws and regulations, history, biblical legends and genealogy, as well as prayers in measured Christian terms.

Because Biblical translations from the original nowadays are accurately expressed, or as nearly so as is possible where there is no exact equivalent, the works of modern scholars have become widely accepted and increasingly popular; but modern Bibles can have little bearing upon a study of material that was produced by masonic writers and compilers whose sources were dated in the 16th and 17th centuries, or earlier.

The biggest influence came from the marginal notes in the *Geneva* Bibles which were published from 1560 onwards and it is worthy of note that this was the Bible of William Shakespeare (1564–1616) and the philosophers of that era. For ten years it was published by Thomas Bodley and, among others who followed, Christopher Barker—'*Printer to the Queenes most Excellent Maiestie*'. It is from the range of *Barker* Bibles that appropriate marginal notes have been taken. The strongly held view is that the theology of the marginal notes in Bibles of that period was not upheld by King James and for that reason, in 1611, he caused the *Authorised Version* of the Bible to be published. Despite this, perhaps even because of it, the *Geneva* Bible was widely favoured and for long afterwards.

For the purpose of this study, where mention is made of 'the original', the text or word in Hebrew is intended. In that respect it has to be borne in mind that one Hebrew word may have a large number of entirely different meanings; that there are only 22 characters or letters in the Hebrew language and they are all consonants; vowels in the words are indicated by an elaborate system known as 'pointing' and that many of the words used in freemasonry have been taken from basic 'unpointed' Hebrew; that Hebrew is read from right to left; that a similarity occurs between several characters and if carelessly written one letter may quite easily be mistaken for another. Thus, with so many built-in hazards it is understandable that mistransliteration, mistranslation, and in consequence mispronunciation of an intended word has at times created non-words and regrettably, at times, nonsense.

When evaluating the propriety of a term or an expression it is well to remember the verbose, repetitive and poetic style of the early writers and compilers of masonic works. However, it should also be borne in mind that it was, at times, balanced by the creation of cryptic forms that were usefully employed to screen the essence of profound thinking, e.g., pictures in stained glass in the cathedrals and churches quite often conveyed the subject of a whole sermon, and pictographs and similar devices as a means of communication were popular among the informed. Much of the fashionable reading of their time has become archaic and is seldom referred to by freemasons of today therefore the intention of a word or a phrase might well be obscured to many brethren.

The object of this examination is to provide perspective for those who wish to understand more of the background from which the modern behaviour in freemasonry has developed and for whom the ceremonial and wording might be much more enriched.

MAHHABONE, MAC-BENACH

These are alternative words and, according to *Jachin and Boaz* (1762) from which these forms have been taken, were used by the Antients and Moderns respectively. The appropriate references are:

'The *Word* is MAHHABONE; or in some Lodges MAC-BENACH'; elsewhere in the book the following footnote appears:

' . . . you whisper . . . MAHHABONE, or as in the Modern Lodges, MAC BENACH . . .'

Jachin and Boaz was used by many brethren as a manual and owing to the high demand was continuously reprinted until the Union was effected. Because of the publicity given by that and similar publications in that period it had much to do with those forms becoming stylised.

Everything points to the fact that a different word was chosen by the Antients in order to emphasise the gap that was to exist between themselves and the premier Grand Lodge, members of which they dubbed as 'Moderns'. However, honour was satisfied when both words received approval and their conjoint use became the custom following the Union of the two Grand Lodges in December 1813.

The words were not invented by members of those Grand Lodges but had been taken from a selection already in being. The source, and in which context they emerged, has still to be discovered although a deal of speculation has been applied to the problem. In a study of this nature it is well to review the various forms and the material in which they appear and the following is representative of what is available:

(a) 'Anoth^{er} they haue called the Mast^{ers} word and is Mahabyn which is allways divided into two words . . . they whisp^{er} in each oth^{ers} eares ye one Maha—the oth^{er} repleys Byn.'
(*Sloane MS*, 3329, c. 1700)

(b) 'The Masters sign is . . . the word matchpin . . . and say Matchpin.'
(*Trinity College Dublin MS.*1711)

14

(c) 'Your first word is *Jachin* and *Boaz* is the answer to it ... Your 2d word is *Magboe* and *Boe* is the answer to it ... Your 3rd word is *Gibboram, Esimberel* is the answer ...
The explanation of our Secrets is as follows
Jachin and *Boaz*, two pillars made by *Heirom*, *Jachin* signifies Strength, and *Boaz* Beautiful, *Magboe* and *Boe* signifies Marrow in the Bone, so is our Secret to be concealed—Tho' there is different opinions of this, yet I prove this the truest Construction.—*Gibboram* and *Simber* signifies the *Gibonites*, who built the city of *Simellon* ...'
(*The Whole Institution of Free-Masons Opened*, 1725)

(d) 'After this the Word *Maughbin* is whisper'd by the youngest Mason to the next, and so on till it comes to the Master, who whispers it to the entered Mason ... Then the entered Mason says what follows:

An enter'd Mason I have been,
Boaz and *Jachin* I have seen;
A Fellow I was sworn most rare,
And I know the Astler, Diamond, and Square:
I know the Master's Part full well,
As honest Maughbin will you tell.

Then the Master says:

If a Master-Mason you would be,
Observe you well the *Rule of Three;*
And what you want in Masonry,
Thy *Mark* and *Maughbin* makes thee free.'
(*A Mason's Examination*, 1723)

Mark in this example has nothing to do with the Mark Degree in Freemasonry but has bearing upon syllable pronunciation of *Mem He* and *Mem Heth*, certain Hebrew characters; but that will be dealt with later.

A similar jingle has initials to indicate the word which is identified as *Machbenah* and for which an explanation is supplied:

(e) 'Ex(aminer)   An Enter'd Prentice I presume you have been.

R(esponder)   *Jachin* and *Boaz* I have seen;
A Master-Mason I was made most rare,
With Diamond, Ashler and the Square.

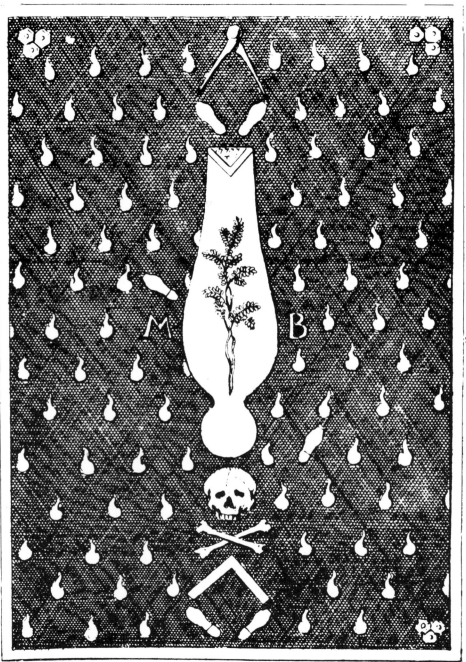

3: Plan of the Master's Lodge (1747)

Ex. If a Master-Mason you would be,
      You must rightly understand the Rule of Three
      And *M.B. shall make you free   *Machbenah
      And what you want in Masonry,
      Shall in this Lodge be shewn to thee.

R.   Good Masonry I understand;
      The keys of all Lodges are at my Command.

. . .   .

Ex.   Give me the Master's Word.
R.   . . . says Machbenah, which signifies *The Builder is
      smitten.*'
      (Samuel Prichard, *Masonry Dissected*, 1730)

The initials M.B. are shown on 'The Master's Floor Plan' reproduced
from *La Désolation Des Entrepreneurs Modernes* (1747) (see Plate 3)
and on the title page of *Le Maçon Démasqué* (1751) which also has
'I. B.' standing for 'Jachin' and 'Boaz' (see Plate 4).

With the exception of *La Réception Mystérieuse* (1738) which has
Machbenah, the French publications between the dates 1737 and 1751
have either *Mak-benak* or *Macbenac* in varying styles; though *L'Ordre
Des Francs-Maçons Trahi* (1745) has an interesting footnote on *Mak-
benak:* 'This is how it should be spelled, & not with two C's.' Interesting
treatment is given to it in *L'Anti-Maçon* (1748) where it is shown in
lettered form in the catechism, with an indication for Pronunciation:
'M.A.K.B.E.N.Ar.K.'.

The following extract justifies consideration:

(f) 'A master stepped forward to raise Adoniram [sic]; he took hold of
     him by the hand, & the first two fingers coming away as a result of
     putrefaction, he informed the Brethren by using the Hebrew word,
     Mac Benac, that is to say, the flesh falls from the bones. As this word
     was the first they spoke, they seized upon it eagerly ([a]) for the word
     of a Master, & it was substituted in place of JEHOVA which had
     been in use till then.

17

LE MAÇON
DÉMASQUÉ,
o u
LE VRAI SECRET DES
FRANCS MAÇONS,

Mis au jour dans toutes ſes parties avec
ſincérité & ſans dèguiſement.

*Sit mihi fas audita Loqui, ſit numine veſtro
Pandere res alta terra & caligine merſas.*
Virg. Ened. 6.

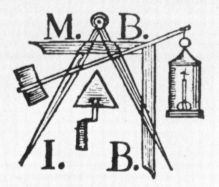

M. B.

I. B.

D. ſi un Franc Maçon ſe perdoit, ou le trouveriéz vous?
R. entre l'équerre, & le Compas.

A LONDRES,

Chés Owen Temple Bar. 1751
Le Prix eſt un Shelling.

4:    Title page of 'Le Maçon Démasqué' (1751)

(a) Note that this adventure is at one and the same time contrary to truth, & to probability: not the slightest trace of it is found in scripture, or in history.'
(*Le Maçon Démasqué*, 1751)

Turning now to the English publications; the alternatives have been quoted from *Jachin & Boaz* (1762) but no meaning or signification was shown in that; two, dated in 1760, should be brought into the picture:

(g) 'The word is Mack-benack but it is seldom pronounced, because it is looked upon as sacred.'
(*A Master Key to Free-Masonry*, 1760)

(h) '... and say MAHHABONE; that is, almost rotten to the bone ...'
(*Three Distinct Knocks*, 1760)

The latter includes a 'Table of Words' in which not only is a signification given but also the Hebrew characters (see Plate 5). Before leaving this selection of the published references that have bearing, we should turn to an extract from the *Graham MS* bearing the date 24 October 1726:

(i) '... we have it by tradition and still some refferance to scripture cause shem ham and Japheth ffor to go to their father noahs grave for to try if they could find anything about him ffor to Lead them to the vertuable secret which this famieous preacher had ... ... Now

The MASTER's Word is MAHHABONE.	כִּחְבֵּן	This fignifies rotten, or decayed almoſt to the Bone. It is the Word that is whifpered in your Ear at the raifing of your Mafter, and is never to be fpoke out ; for they receive it as folemn as the Name of God.

5: Extract from 'Three Distinct Knocks' (1760)

these 3 men had allready agreed that if they did not ffind the very thing it self that the first thing that they found was to be to them as a secret they not Douting but did most ffirmly be Leive that God was able and would allso prove willing through their faith prayer and obediance for to cause what they did find for to prove as vertuable to them as if they had received the secret at ffirst from God himself at its head spring so came to the Grave finding nothing save the dead body all most consumed away takeing a greip at a ffinger it came away so from Joynt to Joynt so to the wrest so to the Elbow so they R Reared up the dead body and supported it setting ffoot to ffoot knee to knee Breast to breast Cheeck to cheeck and hand to back any cryed help o ffather as if they had said o father of heaven help us now for our Earthly ffather cannot so Laid down the dead body again and not knowing what to do—so one said here is yet marrow in this bone and the second said but a dry bone and the third said it stinketh so they agreed for to give it a name as is known to free masonry to this day ... while the two younger brothers of the aforesaid king alboyin disired for to be instructed by him his noble asiance (science) by which he wrought to which he agreed conditionally they were not to discover it without a another to themselves to make a trible voice so they entered oath and he tought them the heorick [theoretical] and practick [practical] part of masonry ...'
(*Early Masonic Catechisms*, Knoop, Jones & Hamer. The text reproduced photographically in *AQC* Vol 50)

In the same year a newspaper advertisement produced the following:

(j)   'This is to give notice, to all Masons who have been made after the Antediluvian manner.

That there will be a Lodge held at the Ship Tavern in Bishopsgate Street tomorrow the 24th of this Instant June, being the Feast of St. John the Baptist, the Forerunner of ... who laid the first parallel Line ... there not being Brethren enough assembled the last year to make a true and perfect Lodge.

There will be several Lectures on Ancient Masonry, particularly on the Signification of the Letter G. and how and after what Manner the Antediluvian Masons form'd their Lodges, shewing what innovations have lately been introduced by the Doctor and some other of the Moderns, with their Tapes, Jacks, Moveable letters, Blazing Stars, &c., to the great Indignity of the Mop and Pail.

There will likewise be a Lecture giving a particular Description of the Temple of Solomon, shewing which way the Fellow Crafts got into the Middle Chamber to receive their Wages, and proving without lettering or giving the first or second, that the two Pillars of the Porch were not cast in the Vale of Jehosaphat but elsewhere; and that neither the Honorary, Apollonian, or Free and Accepted Masons know anything of the matter; with the whole History of the Widow's Son killed by the Blow of a Beetle, afterwards found three Foot East, three Foot West, and three Foot perpendicular, and the necessity there is for a Master to well understand the Rule of Three.

... ...

N.B. The Wax Chandler near Pall Mall will provide three great Lights and a Gormogon to keep off the Cowin and Eves-droppers.

By Order of the Fraternity

Lewis Giblin, M.B.N.'

(*AQC* Vol. 23, Inaugural Address of H. Sadler.

Text reprinted in *Early Masonic Pamphlets*, Knoop, Jones and Hamer.)

Biblical References

There are three references in the Bible which provide the basis upon which this exercise is mounted:

'Ieremiah the tenth, Macbannai the eleventh'
(1 *Chron.* 12,13)

'She bare also . . . and Sheua the father of Machbenah . . .'
(1 *Chron.* 2,49)

'Of the tribe of Gad, Geuel the son of Machi.'
(*Numbers* 13,15)

They have been taken from the *Barker* Bible (1580) and it is in that series of editions we refer to entries in the section headed:

'Two right profitable and fruitful concordances, or large and ample Tables Alphabetical. The first Alphabet of directions to common places, containing all the Hebrew, Caldean, Greeke, Latine, or other strange names, dispersed throughout the whole Bible, conducing to the profitablest things thereof.

Macbannai or Macbauai [sic] *a wretch,* or *my poore sonne,*
or the povertie of understanding
1 *Chron.* 12,13

Machbana Machbenah, *povertie, the smiting of his sonne*
the povertie of understanding, or
the smiting of the builder
1 *Chron.* 2,49

The following appears in the edition dated 1605:

'Machabani, Macbani. *my poore sonne*
1 *Chron.* 12,13

Machi, *poore, or a smiter*
Num. 13,15'

The series of Tables of Biblical Names is stated to have been 'collected by R. F. H.' (Robert F. Herrey) but whence he derived his information is not known. But, in order to keep the subject in proper perspective it is well to examine certain Hebrew words and syllables that are relative and here is a list which includes an explanation or meaning, although it may be but one of many that can be applied:

עני	ANI	Poor
מחי	MACHI	Poor, or smiter
מחה	MACHAH	Blot out, destroy
מכה	MAKKAH	A blow, or smiting
מק	MAQ	Rottenness, or putrid
מה	MAH	What
ה	H(A)	The (definite article)
בנה	BANAH	To build up
בנא	BENA	Build
בו	BEN	Son
ביו	BIN	Understanding
בינה	BINAH	Understanding
בינאי	BONAI / B'NAI	Builder

We are not aware of the exact period when the Hiramic legend was introduced into Freemasonry but we have early dating of the Five Points of Fellowship and the use of a *Word*. The *Barker* Bibles predate our record by over one hundred years and, on the premise that the Hiramic legend was adapted for masonic ceremonial, perhaps following a version of 'Raising' based upon the sons of Noah attempting to revive their father, and possibly a slight mix of both to create a set of circumstances plausible enough for a 'Lost Word' theme, I hold that here was ample material for the literate to introduce a substitute that would convey in cryptic form something of the story. It is even possible that altered forms have arisen because of the understanding of 'better' Hebrew by other literates but certainly corrupt forms have occurred through mistranslations, etc. If we consider the various aspects that are contained in the legends, e.g., Hiram as a widow's son; being one of three Masters, i.e., the 'Rule of Three'; the 'blotting out' of one who 'understood' something that was 'lost' to those attempting the raising; the loss of one who made three to pronounce the *Name* in syllable form, i.e., the 'trible voice'; Hiram as the 'smitten builder'; decaying flesh that figured in both the Noah legend as well as that of Hiram; there is ample reason for the creation of a substitute Word.

We cannot overlook how easily Hebrew can be mistranslated if it is carelessly written, and what a drastic effect this can have. There are several letters that can be taken one for another; as an example take the character *HE* (ה), noting that the left leg does not join at the top, but if this should happen it becomes another character, *HETH* (ח), and instead of being the equivalent of an H in English it is then CH. Thus, if placed at the end of a syllable such as *MAH*, pronounced 'MAR', it becomes *MACH* which has the guttural pronunciation as used in the Scottish for 'LOCH'; however, even that is pronounced by many, below the Borders, as 'LOCK' so it is not difficult to find the *MACH* syllable becoming 'MACK'. The same exercise can be applied to *BENAH* which becomes BENACK. Another approach could alter *MACH* to 'MATCH', and, doubtless because of local dialect or foreign pronunciation, we could expect BYN—BIN—and PIN to be bedfellows; similarly with BOE and BONE.

Here is a list of '*Words*' that have appeared. It is not intended to be complete only to give some idea of permutation or variety:

MAHHABONE	MAGBOE	MAC BENACH	MACHBENAH
MAHABYN	MAUGHBIN	MAKBENAK	MACHBANA
MATCHPIN		MACKBENAK	MACHABANI
		MACKBENACK	
		MACBANNAI	
		MACBANAI	
		MACBANI	
		MACABONA	

There was much scope for a substitute *Word* and whatever may have been introduced as the one, it is evident that the field was wide open for conflicting ideas and that corruption has taken place over the years. It may have been that some of the 'Enlightened' purposely allowed, or created, cryptic forms in order to screen one that had been accepted among themselves which practice would have brought an even higher class into being.

Freemasonry and the Stuarts

In a study such as this it would be appropriate to refer to the writing of Albert G. Mackey, that great masonic lexicographer. In his *Encyclopedia* he wrote that *MACBENAC* was a word introduced into Freemasonry by the supporters of the House of Stuart, stating that MAC is 'son' and BENACH is 'blessed' from the active verb BEANNAICH— 'to bless'. Whilst his translation from the Gaelic and his inguenity in linking that with Freemasonry is commendable his dating does not apply. His case falls because the Word was already there in the Table of Names in the *Barker* Bibles from 1580 onwards with an explanation printed that was much more appropriate to the Craft legend.

AMMI RUHAMAH

This is an Anglicised version of Hebrew words formed from:

הַ	עַ	ח	ר	׳	עַ	צ
HE	MEM	HETH	RESH	YOD	MEM	AYIN

Bible Reference

'Then said God ... Say ye unto your brethren AMMI* and to your sisters RUHAMAH**

*That is, *my people*

**That is, *having obtained mercy* (*Hosea* chap. 2, v. 1)

Meaning or Import

The meaning commonly attributed is as given above which is quoted from the *Barker* Bible dated 1614. The word AMMI is correctly translated but the strict meaning of RUHAMAH is 'pitied' and, according to Robert Young's *Analytical Concordance to the Holy Bible* (Lutterworth Press, USCL, London 8th Edn. 1939) the word is 'A symbolic name of Israel'. The word does not appear in the Hebrew *Index-Lexicon* of that work therefore must be treated as not pure Hebrew.

Pronunciation

Based upon the English rendering of the words:

AMMI   — AHMEE
RUHAMAH   — RU-AR-MAH

A Hebrew pronunciation would treat the first H in RUHAMAH as CH which would introduce a guttural as in the word 'loch'.

Symbolical Application

In the Bible the Jews are frequently referred to as 'my people' and the description of them as 'children of Israel' often occurs. The following is an example where both expressions are combined:

> 'But Pharaoh shall not hearken unto you, that I may lay my hand upon Egypt, and bring forth mine armies, and *my people the children of Israel*, out of the land of Egypt ...' (*Exodus*, chap. 7, 4).

RABBONI

This word is Aramaic, a form of Hebrew among the Semitic languages in use in the Middle East in the Christian era. In Hebrew it would be written thus:

׳	נ	ו	ב	ר
YOD	NUN	VAV	BETH	RESH

Biblical Reference

The word occurs only once in the Bible. It was used as a title of honour by Mary of Magdala (Mary Magdalene) when she addressed Jesus after the resurrection, albeit with incredulity:

> 'Mary . . . said unto him, *Rabboni*, which is to say Master.'
> (*John* 20,16)

Meaning

Exactly as stated in the quotation. The Hebrew word 'Rabbi' would be the equivalent and is written thus:

׳	ב	ר
YOD	BETH	RESH

It signifies 'Teacher' but is usually applied to a teacher of 'the Law', i.e., an ecclesiastic.

Alternatives

The following plural forms have appeared from time to time:

RABBONIM;   RABBANAIM

27

I AM THAT I AM

A statement made by the Almighty to denote a divine status, a positive state of *BEING*, one that is beyond the need of explanation. The expression indicates the unsearchableness of God so that it is more than just existence.

Hebrew

In the original it is set out thus:

ר	שׁ	א		ה	יׄ	ה	א
RESH	SHIN	ALEPH		HE	YOD	HE	ALEPH

		ה	יׄ	ה	א
		HE	YOD	HE	ALEPH

Bible References

The *Barker* Bible (1580) has:

> 'And Moses said unto God, Behold, when I come unto the children of Israel, and shall say unto them, The God of your fathers hath sent me unto you; and they shall say unto me, What is his name? What shall I say unto them?
> And God answered Moses I AM THAT I AM* also he sayhe Thus shalt thou say unto the children of Israel, I AM hath sent me unto you.
> *The God which have ever bene, am, & shall be: the God almightie, by who all things have their being, and the God of mercy mindful of my promes. *Revel.* 1,4'
> (*Exodus* 3,13–14)

The positive statement, I AM, has been built up to 'the Great I am' and links with phrases from the following references:

> 'Thus saith the LORD the King of Israel, and his redeemer the LORD of hosts; I *am* the first, and I *am* the last; and beside me there is no God.'
> (*Isaiah* 44,6)

I am Alpha and Omega, the beginning and the ending, saith the
Lord, which is, and which was, and which is to come, the Almighty
. . .
I am Alpha and Omega, the first and the last . . .
(*Revelations* 1,8–11)

In 1841, in the introduction to *Christian Iconography*, M. Didron
wrote:

'Christianity was the all-powerful influence which, during the centuries intervening between the ninth and seventeenth of our era,
produced in cathedrals, parish churches, and private chapels; in
colleges, abbeys and priories; a profusion almost incredible of
figures, images, and sacred subjects, sculptured, carved painted,
engraved, and even woven into tapestries and costly hangings.
Some large churches, such as those of Chartres, Rheims, Paris,
and Amiens, are adorned with no fewer than two, three, or even four
thousand statues of stone.'

What he said of large churches in France also applied in other
countries. Ten years later his book was translated into English and
published in London (Bohn, 1851) where I have little doubt it was
popular, enabling some freemasons to recognise and understand a little
more of the background.

In the chapter dealing with the Nimbus it is stated:

'The cruciform nimbus is entirely appropriated to the Deity: it is
given more peculiarly to Christ the Saviour and frequently, as in the
Byzantine monuments, as has been already shown, the letters ὁ ὤν, *I
am*, or 'He who is' are inscribed on the branches of the cross.' (p. 46)

In a MS *Guide* which he purchased at Mount Athos, and was duly
translated by his colleague M. P. Durand, he found the following
directions:

'On the cross intersecting the crown (nimbus) of each of the three
persons of the Trinity, the Father, Son, and Holy Ghost, let the

29

following letters be inscribed, ὁ ὤν, for it is by these words that God was pleased to reveal himself to Moses in the burning bush; 'ἐγὼ ἐιμὶ ὁ ὤν.' 'I am that I am', let the letters be thus arranged . . .'

His 'Fig 15' is a 14th century Greek painting of Christ, with a cruciform nimbus with the transverse branches inscribed ὁ ὤν, 'I am'. (See Plate No. 5)

6: A 14th century Greek painting

THE TRIPLE TAU

The tau (pronounced 'taw') is the final character in the Hebrew alphabet and is written thus ת. Dependent upon its employment in a particular word it may be the equivalent of a hard 't' as in the words 'tin' or 'wit', or as a 'th' in the words 'these' or 'with'. Due note should be taken of its use as 'th' as this will arise later.

An allusion is sometimes made to link this character with the biblical account in *Exodus* chap. 12 which describes the commands given to the Israelites for a sacrifice in readiness for the Passover:

> 7. And they shall take of the blood, and strike it on the two side posts and on the upper door post of the houses ...
> 13. And the blood shall be to you for a token upon the houses where ye are; and when I see the blood, I will pass over you, and the plague shall not be upon you to destroy you, when I smite the land of Egypt.
> 29. And it came to pass, that at midnight the LORD smote all the firstborn in the land of Egypt.

The view has been held that the two side posts and the lintel above represents the form of the tau but although that story persists it should fail on two counts, firstly because of the curl, or serif, on the left leg, and secondly that in the early Hebrew scrolls the tau was written as an X, or cross; if one needed to associate that event with a character then the Heth (pronounced '*cheth*' with a commencing guttural) would be more appropriate as that is written thus ח.

When the Hebrew manuscripts were translated first into Greek, then into Latin and from that into English, the tau was interpreted as the letter 't'. In its capital form thus T it has been called 'the Tau Cross', also 'St. Anthony's Cross' (see Plate 7). It is from that letter and that form the Triple Tau has been manufactured by joining three of those letters at their base, one upright and two placed horizontally.

A very different situation occurs in the biblical account in *Ezekiel* (chap. ix, 3–4) which is at a much later stage in the history of the Israelites:

> 3. ... And he called to the man clothed with linen, which had the writer's inkhorn by his side;

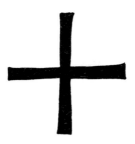

The Greek Cross, Crux immissa quadrata. From this and the Latin Cross the following forms were derived in the middle ages for heraldic purposes:

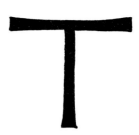

St. Anthony's, or Egyptia Cross; Crux commissa. Als called the Tau Cross, from th Greek letter "T", tau. St. Francis used this as his signatur

The Latin Cross, Crux ordinaria, in early times called God's mark. The most exalted emblem of the Christian faith, the Sign of all Signs. By far the greater number of signs in the Western world are based on the shape, or part of the shape of the Cross, whether they be imperial monograms, masonic signs, family signs, chemical symbols, or trademarks.

The Monogram of Jesus. Instead of the first three Greek letters of the word Jesus, IHC Later the H was regarded as a Latin letter, and the meaning attributed to the monogran

The most widespread and best-known Chrismon.

7: *Various Diagrams from the Book of Signs (1930)*

4. And the LORD said unto him, Go through the midst of the city, through the midst of Jerusalem, and set a mark upon the foreheads of all men that sigh and that cry for all the abominations that be done in the midst thereof.

Where the words 'set a mark' occur in that translation, the original Hebrew scrolls have the word 'tau', spelt with a Tau and a Vav thus ות (reading from right to left). By virtue of the biblical accounts the letter T became associated with faith in the Almighty and preservation of life.

We now have to look at an entirely separate symbol which has occurred in Christian symbolism, one with which the Triple Tau is also associated; it is a Latin Cross surmounted, superimposed, or resting upon the letter H (see diagram). It has been described as 'Holiness supporting Trinity' and an early example of that occurred in *The Trinity College, Dublin MS*, dated 1711, where it is to be seen heading a short masonic catechism (see Plate 8). It was reproduced by Knoop, Jones and Hamer in *Early Masonic Catechisms* (Manchester University Press, 1943, p. 63). Variations of that symbol, and its use, are prolific (see diagrams). It commenced as a monogram which abbreviated a mixture of Latin and Greek to signify the name Jesus. Among the meanings given to it are '*Jesus Hominum Salvator*' ('Jesus Saviour of Mankind') and '*In Hoc Signo*' ('By this sign shalt thou conquer'). According to the Oxford *Dictionary of the Christian Church Cross*, in the Middle Ages it was widely used among the Dominicans and later became used by the Jesuits who gave it the interpretation '*Jesus Habemus Socium*' ('We have Jesus as our Companion'). The letters I and J are interchangeable although there is no J in the Greek language. Another Christian symbol is the Latin Cross superimposed upon the letter X and is a combination of the two Greek letters *rho*, or P, and *chi*, or X and, being the first two letters of the Greek word for Christ making what is known as the '*Labarum*'. This is mentioned only in passing but it has no bearing on our subject.

However, the Greek letter T shown above the letter H, forming a combination of 'th' mentioned above and therefore a use of the Hebrew tau, finds an official use in *The Charter of Compact*, the document by which the first Grand Chapter for the Royal Arch was set up at the Turk's Head, in Greek Street, London, on 22nd July 1766. Here is the appropriate extract:

... THIRDLY That every Companion shall wear according to ancient custom an Apron indented with Crimson, and the Badge ⊞ properly displayed thereon. ...

Various Royal Arch manuscripts, undated but attributed to the end of the 18th century and early 19th, have references to that symbol and here are three examples:

(1) ... the compound character ⊞ which signifies '*Templum Hierosolimi*' and is always held as the R.A. Masons' badge, by which the wearer acknowledges himself a servant of the true God who had there established his true worship and to whose service that great Temple was dedicated. ... (*Prudence MS.* G.L. Library ref: BE 396 PRU)

(2) What was the next thing you found?
     The R.A. signature ⊞ i.e., Holiness supporting Trinity, the signature of a R.A. summons, which we are bound to obey by the tenor of our Ob. to obey. Should we neglect to answer or obey our next summons will be signed ⊞E, Hiram King of Tyre, Excellent; which if we neglect, it is the power of the Chapter to render us incapable ever to enter the Chapter after.
     (*Deptford MS.* St. Georges Chapter, G.L. library ref: BE 395 SA1)

(3) On the base of this Pedestal is the letter G which signifies ... a common name for all masons that are Masters of their business. ... Under these were found the compound character TH, which signifies Templum Hierosolima, or Temple of Jerusalem and is always used as a part of the R.A. Masons' signature by which the wearer acknowledges himself a servant of the true God, who had there established his worship and to whose service the Glorious Temple was erected. (*Tunnah MS.* G.L. library ref: BE210 TUN)

The Triple Tau then started life as a very distinct T over an equally distinct H and those explanations were given to it as a compound character. The *Tunnah MS* is almost identical with what was used by William Finch whose work was widespread in the early part of the 19th century and was copied by Richard Carlile in 1825 and perpetuated in all editions up to 1850, *but not referred to as a Triple Tau*.

Following the meetings of the Chapter of Promulgation, set up to effect a uniformity of ritual and procedure in the Royal Arch in 1834/5, George Claret supplied manuscript ritual for the Royal Arch from

8: THE TRINITY COLLEGE, DUBLIN, MS., 1711

This short catechism, which is in the Trinity College, Dublin, Library [T.C.D.MS. I, 4, 18], is contained in one of the volumes of collected papers of Sir Thomas Molyneux (1661–1733), a famous Dublin doctor and scientist. It is written on one side of a single folio sheet, about $11\frac{3}{4}"\times 7\frac{1}{2}"$, and was originally folded into four, about $3"\times 7\frac{1}{2}"$; across the top the folded document was endorsed 'Free Masonry Feb: 1711'. To judge from the photostat made in 1937, the endorsement is in a different hand from the body of the text, the 'M', the 's', and the 'y' of 'Masonry' in the endorsement differing considerably from the same letters in the body of the text. The MS. has been put away in a place of safety, and our observation, based on the photostat, cannot at present be checkd by reference to the original. Nor can it be ascertained, by comparison with other documents, whether either the body of the text, or the endorsement, was written by Sir Thomas Molyneux himself. If either was, we surmise that it was the endorsement. The catechism is the earliest known MS. to recognize three classes of mason, each with its own secrets. It was printed in *Trans. Lodge of Research No. CC, Dublin,* 1924. Our transcript is made from a photostat. See Introduction, pp. 10, 21 above.

Under no less a penalty

Question. W^t manner of man are you? Answer. I am a mason.

Q. How shall I know that? A. By ye signs, tokens, & points of my entry.

Q. Where were you entered? A. In a full, & perfect lodge.

Q. W^t makes a full, & perfect lodge? A. three masters, 3 fellow craftsmen, & 3 enterprentices.

Q. How stands y^r lodge? A. East, & west like ye temple of Jerusalem.

Q. Where sits ye master? A. In a Chair of bone in ye middle of a four square pavement.

1838. His first printed Royal Arch manual appeared in 1845, probably it did not justify printing before that date owing to a limited demand. It is in that work we have positive reference to the Triple Tau, as follows:

> ... There was likewise a Triple Tau, or Letter T, a mark or character affixed to the summonses of R.A. Masons, when summoned on other than usual occasions. The Triple Tau, or letter T, is translated

from the Hebrew, a mark or sign spoken of by Ezekiel, when it was said to the man with the writer's inkhorn ... In ancient times this mark was placed on the forehead of all those who were acquitted by their judges, as a proof of their innocence; and military commanders caused a T to be placed on all those who had escaped unhurt from the field of battle, denoting that they were in perfect life. It has therefore ever been considered the mark of life. The union of the three Ts alludes to the grand tri-union of the Deity ...

What was stated in the *Charter of Compact* to be the Royal Arch Badge lost its individuality when the letter T over the letter H joined together at the base and became three letters T. When that happened is not recorded and no authority can be found but it might well have stemmed from the deliberations of the Chapter of Promulgation of 1834/5. The earlier T over H symbol, that is shown on the Pedestal used in Swalwell chapter   (see Plate 9) ceased to be and with it went the earlier attributions and its Christian connotation. It became a mathematical exercise and is described in the Symbolical lecture as having:

> ... two right angles at each of its exterior lines and two in the centre; in all, eight right angles, corresponding in number with those contained in the four triangles; for the three angles of every triangle are together equal to two right angles.

Also linked in that exploit in geometry are the six lights, the Jewel of the Order, and the Platonic Bodies.

The process of change has dealt harshly with the ideas and ideals which motivated those of the Order who were responsible for the development of the early forms of Royal Arch ritual and procedure.

9: A Modern Triple Tau

10: *T over H on miniature pedestal, Swalwell Chapter, Durham*

MOSES, AARON AND ELEAZAR

Family Relationship

A family relationship existed between these Biblical personalities; Aaron was Moses' brother and Eleazar was Aaron's third son.

Moses

Moses was so named by a daughter of Pharaoh:

> 'And she called his name Moses* . . . because I drew him out of the water.
>
> *That is, *drawn out*'
> (*Exodus* 2,10)

Moses was commissioned by the Almighty to lead his people from Egyptian slavery and for this purpose was given an authority that was to be demonstrated by his power to produce signs beyond normal. Moses pleaded inadequacy of speech but in this was granted assistance through the appointment of his brother Aaron:

> 'And Moses said unto the LORD . . . I *am* not eloquent . . . I *am* slow of speech, and of a slow tongue. . . . And the anger of the LORD was kindled against Moses and he said, *Is* not Aaron the Levite thy brother? I know that he can speak well . . . And he shall be thy spokesman unto the people . . . And thou shalt take this rod in thine hands, wherewith thou shalt do signs.'
> (*Exodus* 4,10–17)

Later in life he became known as 'The Lawgiver', and there are several references regarding this:

> 'And Moses wrote this law, and delivered it unto the priests the sons of Levi, which bare the ark of the covenant of the LORD, and unto the elders of Israel.
> (*Deuteronomy* 31,9)

Only be thou strong and very courageous, that thou mayest observe
to do according to all the law, which Moses my servant commanded
thee.'
(*Joshua* 1,7)

Aaron

The meaning of this name in Hebrew is 'Enlightened'. Aaron was the
first High Priest of the Jews and although divinely appointed to assist
Moses remained subordinate.

Eleazar

In Hebrew the name means 'God hath helped'. Eleazar was the third
son of Aaron whom he succeeded in the office of High Priest. This set
up a sacerdotal line which was to include Zadok (11th in descent from
Aaron) the priest who anointed Solomon as King of Israel:

'And Zadok the priest took an horn of oil out of the tabernacle, and
anointed Solomon: And they blew the trumpet, and all the people
said, God save King Solomon.'
(1 *Kings* 1,39)

HOLINESS TO THE LORD

This expression is a translation from the Hebrew:

ה	ו	ה	׳	ל	שׁ	ר	ק
HE	VAV	HE	YOD	LAMED	SHIN	DALETH	QOPH

The Anglicised version of the original is "KODESH La ADONAI".

Meaning

The Hebrew characters *YOD HE VAV HE* constitute 'The Ineffable *NAME*' and, with four exceptions, wherever the 'Name' appears the rendering in the Bible is 'LORD' always printed in capital letters. For a development of this subject see under 'JEHOVAH' later in this study.

Bible References

> 'And thou shalt make a plate *of* pure gold, and grave upon it, like the engraving of a signet, HOLINESS TO THE LORD.
> And thou shalt put it on a blue lace, that it may be upon the miter; upon the forfront of the miter it shall be.
> And it shall be upon Aaron's forehead ...
> (*Exodus* 28,36–8)

The characters appear on the miniature mitre surmounting the sceptre borne by a Third Principal.

Inclusion in the Arms of Grand Lodge

Clear detail of the Hebrew is to be seen in the reproduction of the Arms of Grand Lodge in the frontispiece of the *Book of Constitutions* [see Plate 11].

The legend appeared in crudely drawn Hebrew characters above the Ark of the Covenant depicted in the Arms of the Antients' Grand Lodge (1751–1813). These Arms were combined with those of the premier Grand Lodge (1717–1813) to form the central blazon of the Arms adopted by the United Grand Lodge of England following the Union of those two Grand Lodges in December 1813.

11:   The Arms of The United Grand Lodge of England

GIBLIM

This is a manufactured word which conveys the plural form of GIBLI.
The Hebrew for it is:

ם	׳	ל	ב	ג
(Final) MEM	YOD	LAMED	BETH	GIMEL

It was applied to the inhabitants of the biblical city of Gebal which was
situated on the coast of Lebanon, north of Sidon. The word 'Giblites'
was an early form but perhaps a better word would have been
'Gebalites'.

Bible References

The following is taken from the *Barker* Bible of 1580:

> 'And the king commanded them, and they brought great stones,
> costly stones, to make the foundation of the house, even hewed
> stones.
>
> And Salomons workemen, and the workemen of Hiram, and the
> *masons hewed and prepared timber and stones for the building of
> the house.
>
> *The Ebrewe word is Giblim, which some say were excellent
> masons.'
> (1 *Kings* 5,17–18)

A later *Barker* Bible (1614) had:

> 'And Solomon's builders and Hirams builders did hew *them*, and the
> *stone-squarers . . .
>
> *Or Giblites as Ezek. 27,9'

The reference indicated in *Ezekiel* is: 'the ancients of Gebal and the wise
men thereof . . .'

The word 'Giblites' occurs also in the Book of Joshua:

> 'And the land of the Giblites, and all Lebanon, toward the sun rising, from Baal-gad under Mount Hermon unto the entering into Hamath.'
> (*Joshua* 13,5)

Meaning

The direct connection with the building of Solomon's Temple is its importance. The attributed meaning is 'Excellent Mason' or 'Stone-squarer' and the source is quoted above. However, the singular is not correct.

Pronunciation

The hard G is used, as the G in 'Gift'.

Corrupt Forms

The following corrupt forms have appeared in printed works:

GIBLUM GIBLEM GIBELEM GIBALEM GHIBLIM CHIBBELUM

There is every possibility that dialect and foreign pronunciation has had an influence on some.

EL ELOHE ISRAEL

The Anglicised version from the Hebrew characters:

'	ה	ל	א		ל	א
YOD	HE	LAMED	ALEPH		LAMED	ALEPH

ל	א	ר	שׁ	'
LAMED	ALEPH	RESH	SHIN	YOD

Bible Reference

From the *Barker* Bible (1614) we have:

> 'And he erected there an altar, and called it El-elohe-Israel*
> *That is, *God the God of Israel.*'
> (*Genesis* 33,20)

Meaning

Exactly as stated in the marginal note above:

> God, the God of Israel

Introduction of the Word Israel

'Israel' was the new name given to Jacob by the angel with whom he had wrestled in the night:

> 'And he said unto him, What is thy name? and he said, Jacob. And he said Thy name shall be called no more Jacob, but Israel: for as a prince hast thou power with God, and with men, and hast prevailed'
> (*Genesis* 32,27–8)

Jacob's successors were then known as 'the Children of Israel and it became the name of the nation of which he was the third Patriarch, in succession to Abraham and Isaac. By association it became the name of the land they occupied after the Wanderings in the Wilderness of Sinai following the Exodus from Egypt.

BERITH

An Anglicised version of the Hebrew word thus:

ת	י	ר	ב
TAU	YOD	RESH	BETH

Meaning or Import

The word means 'Covenant'.

Bible References

It appears 273 times in the *Authorised Version* and the first use is:

> 'God said unto Noah . . . But with thee will I establish my covenant
> . . .'
> (*Genesis* 6,18)

The following is an important reference:

> '. . . And he wrote upon the tables the words of the covenant, the
> ten* commandments.'
> *or wordes [sic]
> (*Exodus* 34,28)

That particular marginal note from the *Barker* Bible dated 1580 has a
bearing upon the following reading and enables one to understand its
meaning:

> 'According to the word [i.e., commandments] that I covenanted with
> you, when ye came out of Egypt, so my spirit remaineth among you;
> fear ye not.'
> (*Haggai* 2,5)

Pronunciation

The English E is not used. The pronunciation of the Hebrew *TAU* (ת) is
as a T, but because it is transcribed in English as TH that has become
the common but incorrect pronunciation.
'B'rit' is usually heard as 'B'rith'.

45

EL SHADDAI

An expression which conveys the omnipotence of God, from the Hebrew as follows:

'	ר	שׁ		ל	א
YOD	DALETH	SHIN		LAMED	ALEPH

Meaning or Import

'God Almighty'

Bible References

There are numerous references in the Bible but the one best suited for this study is:

> 'And I appeared unto Abraham, to Izhak and to Jaakob by *the name of* *Almightie God: but by my name **Jehovah was I not known to them.
>
> *or, *all sufficient*
> **whereby he signifieth that he will performe in deede that which he promised to their fathers: for this Name declareth that he is constant, and will performe his promes.'
> (*Exodus* 6,3)

The two words have been transposed in that version of the 1580 *Barker* Bible, (whereas the *Authorised Version* has 'God Almighty', which follows the Hebrew form). The marginal note provides us with yet another recognisable expression.

Pronunciation

Unfortunately the second word so often receives the treatment given to other words of similar character such as Haggai and Sinai. The correct pronunciation should be 'EL SHAD-EYE' as, indeed, should the former words be 'HAG-EYE and 'SIGN-EYE' respectively.

NEDER

A Hebrew word formed from:

ר	ד	נ
RESH	DALETH	NUN

Meaning or Import

The literal meaning is 'A vow'.

Bible References

There are numerous references in the Bible but the following is best suited:

> 'And Jacob vowed a vow, saying, If God will be with me, and will keep me in this way that I go, and will give me bread to eat, and raiment to put on: So that I come again to my fathers house in peace: then shall the LORD be my God. And this stone, which I have set *for* a pillar, shall be God's house: and of all that thou shalt give me, I will surely give the tenth unto thee.'
> (*Genesis* 28, 20–22)

Pronunciation

The proper pronunciation is 'Nee-der'. Because of mispronunciation the word has been confused with two others: 'NADAR' which is another version of the Hebrew word, meaning 'to vow' or 'vowed to', heard as 'NAY-DAR'; and 'NADIR' heard either as 'NAR-DEAR' or 'NAY-DEAR' which is an English word indicating the opposite to Zenith.

JEHOVAH

This is a manufactured word which stands for the intention of the following Hebrew characters:

ה	ו	ה	י
HE	VAV	HE	YOD

But, this is the personal *Name* of the Most High. It is referred to as 'Ha Shem', 'The Name', 'The Ineffable Name' and 'The Tetragrammaton'.

Bible References

One reference which has been given under 'EL SHADDAI' is applicable, others include:

'That *men* may know, that thou whose name alone is JEHOVAH art
the Most High over all the earth.'
(*Psalm* 83,18)

'. . . for the LORD JEHOVAH *is* my strength and *my* song, he also is
become my salvation.'
(*Isaiah* 12,2)

'. . . Trust ye in the LORD for ever: for in the LORD JEHOVAH *is*
everlasting strength.'
(*Isaiah* 26,4)

'. . . by thee only will we make mention of thy name.'
(*Isaiah* 26,13)

Derivation and Variations

The Name of the Most High was, and is, sacrosanct and was pronounced only by the priesthood:

'And he that blasphemeth the name of the LORD, he shall surely be
put to death, *and* all the congregation shall certainly stone him . . .'
(*Leviticus* 24,16)

' ... Then shall he say, Hold thy tongue: for we may not make
mention of the name of the LORD.'
(*Amos* 6,10)

Because of this limitation, and the absence of vowel indication in
classical, basic unpointed Hebrew the Pronunciation was lost. When-
ever the *Name* appears in the original, Jews will substitute the word
ADONAI or will say either 'Ha Shem' or 'The Name'. With the
exception of the four instances that have been quoted from the
Authorised Version the Tetragrammaton is not translated as JEHO-
VAH but as LORD and is then always printed in capital letters.

The word JEHOVAH was manufactured by inserting the vowels
from the Hebrew pointing for the word ADONAI. Among alternative
versions are JAHWEH and JAHWE.

The Word in The Craft

Although the word appears in the Craft and is mentioned in an
explanation there is no evidence that it was actually used in ritual or
ceremonial. It appears in the *Master's Floor Plan* printed in several 18th
century French publications (see Plates 11 and 12). An interesting one
is reproduced in *La Désolation des Entrepreneurs Modernes du Temple
de Jerusalem* (1747), (see Plate No. 3). Apart from the poorly drawn,
pointed Hebrew, this one has the initials 'M. B.', a matter which was
dealt with under the '*Mahhabone, Mach Benah*' section. The common
form of explanation is given as follows:

'The Master [= M.M.] had only a word to distinguish him from
those I have been discussing, which was JEHOVA [or, in some
JEOVA] but that was changed after the death of Adoniram [sic].'
(*Le Catéchism Des Francs-Maçons*, 1744)

12:    Plan of the Master's Lodge (1744)

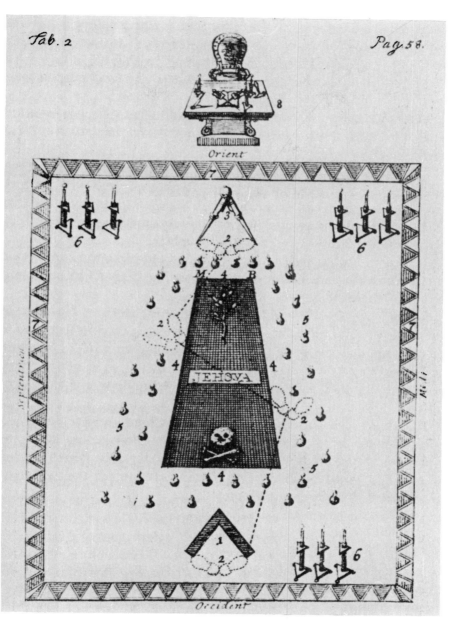

13: *Drawing for the Master's Lodge (1751)*

Biblical References

The word JAH is a contraction of the word JEHOVAH but nevertheless is a word in its own right. It is used also as a prefix or suffix in other words and is formed from the first and second letters of the Tetragrammaton, *JOD HE*. It occurs 24 times in the original as a proper Name but only once in the English translation. In the *Barker* Bible (1589) it has an interesting marginal note as follows:

'Sing unto God, sing praises to his Name extol him that rideth on the heavens by his name *JAH, and rejoice before him.'

*IAH and IEHOUAH are the names of God which doe signify his effence and majestie incomprehensible, so that hereby is declared that all idoles are but vanitie, and that the God of Israel is the only true God.'
(*Psalm* 68, 4)

As a suffix it is extensively used and the following are but examples:

Isaiah	—	Jah is helper (or salvation)
Hilkiah	—	Jah is protection
Nehemiah	—	Jah is comfort
Adonijah	—	Jah is my Lord
Elijah	—	My God is Jah

Heading on Charters

The word was much used in the heading of Charters issued in 1769 by Grand Chapter:

'In the Name of the Grand Architect of the Universe
The Almighty I A H.'

It was also used on various Masonic Certificates issued by private Lodges, as well as on Lodge jewels; probably because it was concise.

Pronunciation

Because there is no J in Hebrew the strict pronunciation for both JEHOVAH and JAH should be *YEHOVAH* and *YAH* but because the Anglicised form of the word has J and not Y the common pronunciation is with a hard J as in John.

JAH BUL ON

These three syllables have been compounded to manufacture a word which was described thus in an early *MS* (c. 1796):

'... what is used for the sacred word itself ..., containing the essence of all language and probably neither to be fully comprehended by human wisdom nor clearly pronounced by the voice and tongue of man.'

It is possible that the introduction of a manufactured word, given a meaning of divine nature, through Biblical connection, and the concise form of The '*Name*', was an attempt to lay stress on the status of the Ineffable Name and the fact of the lost pronunciation. Variations of the three syllables have appeared and they include JAO BUL ON, JAH BEL ON, or permutations of those, but the common form is the one shown as the heading.

Meanings

The word JAH has been dealt with under its own heading.

BUL　This is a Hebrew word written thus:

ל	ו	ב
LAMED	VAV	BETH

It has at least three meanings, one of which is the name of the eighth month in the Hebrew calendar. It occurs only once in the Bible, in an account of the completion of Solomon's Temple:

'And in the eleventh year, in the month BUL, which *is* the eighth month, was the house finished throughout all the parts thereof, and according to all the fashion of it. So was he seven years in building it.'
(1 *Kings* 6,38)

However, BUL is stated to be a compound word itself and consists of 'the preposition BETH, in or on, and UL, heaven or high' so for that reason it must be subjected to a closer examination.

BETH This is the name of the second character in the Hebrew alphabet but it bears the name only if it is unpointed otherwise it is known as *BAYITH:*

(2) BAYITH   (1) BETH

The pointed character indicates that it is to be used as a hard B whereas the *BETH* is used as a V, but they are interchangeable and often a word will have two forms such as Abraham or Avraham.

In addition to it being the name of the second letter in the Hebrew alphabet and a preposition with meanings 'in or on', the word *BETH* also means 'House' or 'Place' and in this sense has connotation with 'Temple'.

UL. There is no U in Hebrew but this word would be expressed in two different ways *EL* or *AL* and would be written thus:

(2) LAMED   AYIN   (1) LAMED   ALEPH

Among its many applications example (1) means 'God' and as such is used 212 times in the Bible, amongst which is 'El-elohe-Israel' and has been dealt with herein. It may well be that because of the divine implication or content in that part of the word, the syllable BEL was adopted in preference to the syllable BUL. The danger there was the introduction to this exercise of the name of the Babylonian pagan god BEL as mentioned in the following:

'Bel boweth down, Nebo stoopeth, their idols were upon the beasts and upon the cattle . . .'
(*Isaiah* 46,1)

'. . . publish, *and* conceal not: say, Babylon is taken, Bel is confounded, Merodach is broken in pieces: her idols are confounded, her images are broken in pieces.'
(*Jeremiah* 50,2)

Bel was one of a triad of gods of that time and was deemed a father god, a creator, by those worshippers.

Example (2) also has many applications that include 'GOD' and it occurs as a syllable in many names:

Eldad	—	Loved of God
Elealeh	—	God goes up, or is exalted
Eleazer	—	God hath helped, or, is a helper
Elijah	—	Jehovah is my God, or, God himself
Eliab	—	God is father
Bethel	—	House of God

The word also has such meanings as 'high—higher—most high—uppermost' and from a combination of certain meanings from both examples one can quite easily produce 'God on high', 'God most high', or 'Most High God'.

Biblical References

In the original both examples may be found and the expression 'LORD in Heaven, or on High' is in keeping with such descriptions used throughout the Bible of which the following is but a sample:

> ... Blessed *be* Abraham of the most high God, possessor of heaven and earth.
> (*Genesis* 14,19)

> 'The LORD God of heaven, which took me from my father's house and from the land of my kindred ...'
> (*Genesis* 24,7)

> '... till thou know that the most High ruleth in the kingdom of men, and giveth it to whomsoever he will.'
> (*Daniel* 4,25)

> 'Mine eye trickled down, and ceaseth not, without intermission. Till the LORD look down, and behold from heaven.'
> (*Lamentations* 3,49 & 50)

'Glory to God in the highest, and on earth peace, good will towards men.'
(*Luke* 2,14)

ON. This was the name of the capital of Lower Egypt in the Old Testament period. Later it was re-named Beth-Shemesh—'House of the Sun' and later still, under the Ptolemies, named Heliopolis—'City of the Sun', which name it bears today.

In Hebrew the word means 'sun' and is thus expressed:

ן   '   א

NUN   YOD   ALEPH

The only connection this can possibly have with the compound word in question is the association with Joseph.

Biblical References

'And he [the Pharaoh] gave him to wife Asenath the daughter of Poti-pherah priest [or prince] of ON: and Joseph went out over *all* the land of Egypt.'
(*Genesis* 41,45)

'And unto Joseph in the land of Egypt were born Manasseh and Ephraim which Asenath the daughter of Poti-pherah priest [or prince] of ON bare unto him.'
(*Genesis* 46,20)

'He shall break also the images of Beth-Shemesh, that *is* in the land of Egypt: and the houses of the gods of the Egyptians shall burn with fire.'
(*Jeremiah* 43,13)

The name of the city provides a useful syllable for the compound word but it is also, by association, an opportunity to remember that Joseph was a child of the Patriarch Jacob's old age. He was sold by his brothers to certain traders and taken into Egypt where his talents enabled him to attain high standing in favour with the Pharaoh. His two sons

Manasseh and Ephraim were blessed by the Patriarch Jacob and through this adoption each received status as separate tribes which were eventually to inherit shares of the land of Israel as members of the Twelve. It would not have bearing upon sun-worship but upon the Patriarchal connection, and from that aspect of posterity the development of the ancient faith, culminating in the building of the successive Temples at Jerusalem.

AB BAL – AL BAL – LAB BAL

These are Anglicised Hebrew words which have been taken to represent the following: 'Father Lord, Word Lord, Spirit Lord.' They are now examined separately but still as components of that expression.

BAL = Lord

This word is linked with all three, and should be formed from the following Hebrew characters:

ל	ע	ב
LAMED	AYIN	BETH

The literal English transcription for that is BAL but it is usually printed as *Ba'al.*

Meaning

The meaning of the word is 'Lord, Master, Possessor'. It has five applications in the Bible:

1 It is the name of an idol that was worshipped by Caananites, Tyrians, and Phoenicians.
2 It is the name of a biblical city (*Chron.* 4,33)
3 The name of a descendant of Reuben (1 *Chron.* 5,5)
4 The name of a descendant of Benjamin (1 *Chron.* 8,30)
5 Considerable use as a prefix in the construction of titles and place names.

Much resentment has arisen because of the connection of the word with the name of a pagan god but this must have been ignored by the early writers who were swayed by example 5, above. When used in a title it is always interpreted as 'Lord of . . .' e.g., Ba'al Gad which means 'Lord of Fortune' (*Joshua* 11,17) or Ba'al Hamon—'Lord of the Multitude' (*Song of Solomon* 8,11) and many others in the Bible.

In the sense that Lord when printed in the Bible as LORD signifies the Tetragrammaton then an allusion to The Almighty can be seen.

Royal Arch Treatment

The combination of Hebrew characters *Aleph*, *Beth*, and *Lamed* is said to correspond to the A, B and L of the English alphabet, but regrettably the statement cannot be supported in regard to the *Aleph*. It does not equate with the English letter A for its function is to serve as a preparation for the letter which follows, even as the letter H is used in the word 'Honour'; it is an aspiration only. Placed before a *Lamed*, or letter L, it would produce the sound only of that letter whereas if the *Ayin* took the place before the *Lamed* it would have the effect of the English letter A to produce AL, although the pronunciation would favour 'Ail'. A modern example is shown in the name of the Israeli Airline EL AL. In Hebrew, the first word EL, although written in opposite sequence of right to left, has *Aleph Lamed* making EL and the second word written *Ayin Lamed* makes 'AL'.

The pronunciation, in English, for *Beth*, *Aleph*, and *Lamed* therefore is BEL and not BAL and it is a word which appears in various early Royal Arch manuscripts. Both Isaiah and Jeremiah wrote denouncing the pagan god of that name in their efforts to preserve faith in their people:

> BEL boweth down, Nebo stoopeth, their idols were upon the beasts, and upon the cattle. (*Isaiah* chap. 46,1) Say Babylon is taken, Bel is confounded, Merodach is broken in pieces; her idols are confounded, her images are broken in pieces. (*Jeremiah* chap. 50,2)
>
> And I will punish Bel in Babylon ... (*Jeremiah* chap. 51,44)

The connection with the pagan god bearing that name has been the cause of dissension as it detracts from the original purpose, which itself became complicated in the early 19th century.

AB = Father

The Hebrew word for Father is AB which is formed thus:

ב   א
BETH   ALEPH

The essence of so much that is in Freemasonry springs from the acknowledgement of the Fatherhood of God and the Brotherhood of man and this was well stated in the following:

'Have we not all one father? Hath not one God created us ...'
(*Malachi* 2,10)

Indication of a divine Sonship was given in the Old Testament:

'For unto us a Child is born, unto us a Son is given, and the government shall be upon his shoulder: his name shall be called Wonderful, Counsellor, The mighty God, The everlasting Father, The Prince of Peace.
Of the increase of *his* government and peace *there shall be* no end, upon the throne of David, and upon his kingdom, to order it, and to establish it with judgment and with justice from henceforth even for ever. The zeal of the LORD of hosts will perform this.'
(*Isaiah* 9,6–7)

But the ritual compilers drew from the Bible as a whole, both New as well as Old Testaments, hence we find the evidence which refers to the following:

'After this manner therefore pray ye, 'Our Father which art in heaven, Hallowed be thy Name ...'
(*Matthew* 6,9)

And the identical sentiment expressed by Malachi appearing in the following:

'Jesus saith ... go to my brethren, and say unto them, I ascend unto my Father, and to your Father, and *to* my God and your God.'
(*John* 20,17)

AL = Word

The Hebrew word for God is *EL* (plural *ELOHIM*) and it is shown thus:

61

ל   א

LAMED   ALEPH

In the sense that God gave his Commandments (*Words*) to Moses he could be styled 'WORD LORD'. A further reference is to be found as follows:

> 'According to the word that I covenanted with you when ye came out of Egypt, so my spirit remaineth among you':
> (*Haggai* 2,5)

The following frequently appeared on Chapter Certificates and in Masonic writings:

> 'In the beginning was the Word, and the Word was with God, and the Word was God.'
> (*John* 1,1)

Direct reference to this was made in a broadsheet dated 1725:

> 'Yet for all this I want the primitive Word, I answer it was God in six Terminations, to wit I am, and *Johova* is the answer to it . . . for proof read the first of the first of St John.'
> (*The Whole Institutions of Free-Masons Opened*, Dublin, 1725)

further reference however is to be found in this quotation:

> '. . . and his name is called The Word of God.'
> (*Revelations* 19,13)

LAB = *Spirit*

LAB is a Hebrew word formed from:

ב   ל

BETH   LAMED

This is a loose transcription for 'heart' which would be better expressed as LEB or LEV. The word LAB does have other meanings amongst which are 'midst—understanding—mind—wisdom', but in the Bible it is overwhelmingly used as heart.

According to Scripture actions are inspired from the heart and are measured in this manner by the Almighty:

> '... man looketh on the outward appearance but the LORD looketh on the heart.'
> (*Samuel* 16,7)

Thus, if an action is a manifestation prompted from the heart, then the heart being the source could be matched with the spirit; it was a very small step in poetical thinking and could be the means of linking with the following:

> 'God is a Spirit: and they that worship him must worship him in spirit and in truth.'
> (*John* 4,24)

> 'For as many as are led by the Spirit of God, they are the sons of God. For ye have not received the spirit of bondage again to fear: but ye have received the Spirit of adoption, whereby we cry, Abba, Father. The Spirit itself beareth witness with our Spirit, that we are the children of God.'
> (*Romans* 8, 14–16)

The exercise using the characters at the angles of the Triangle may be deemed to have been inspired from the following Biblical extract:

> 'For there are three that bear record in heaven, the Father, the Word, and the Holy Ghost: and these three are one.'
> (1 *John* 5,7)

Nothing is on record regarding the source, nor the reason for the adoption of the Hebrew characters at the angles of the triangle. But, in a recent discussion with a close colleague, E. Comp. Harry Mendoza, also a Past Master of Quatuor Coronati Lodge, a Past Prestonian Lecturer, and a keen scholar in the Royal Arch, it was posed that by substituting the initials of the Hebrew equivalent words for the Latin which is used in the Trinitarian device, the example for which in this book has been taken from the *Salisbury Missal* and shown as Plate No 14, the characters Aleph, Beth, and Lamed can be produced thus:

Pater	= Father	= **Ab**
Filius	= Son (Word)	= **Be**n
Spiritus	= Spirit	= **Le**b (heart or spirit)

The transpositioning of these characters tends further to obscure the Trinitarian purpose of the original design and an exercise of that nature would have been much in keeping with the thoughts and attitudes of the early 19th century ritual compilers.

Christian Iconography

The permutation of the Hebrew characters follows a format that has long been used to convey the principle of Divine *Trinity in Unity* propagated by the Christian church and cryptically portrayed by such symbols. The reproduction from the *Salisbury Missal* of 1534 supplies a perfectly clear example (see Plate No 14). The dogma that is there stated is:

> 'The Father is not the Son, the Father is not the Holy Spirit, the Holy Spirit is not the Son. The Father is God, the Son is God, the Holy Spirit is God.'

This aspect was not neglected by a Latin Bible date 1640, the frontispiece of which is reproduced herewith (see Plate No 15). In this we can note the central feature as 'The *Name*'—the Tetragrammaton. Other interesting features are worth noting: The central characters depicted on each side of the title panel are Moses and King David. At each corner, reading clockwise from top left, are the four Evangelists, St Matthew, St Mark, St Luke, and St John and clearly shown in attendance with them are the representative symbols of an Angel (Man), Lion, Ox, and an Eagle, which theme is brought into prominence as the devices on the Principal Banners. The roundel at the

14: Trinitarian device from 'Salisbury Missal' (1534)

15: Title page of Bible in Latin (1640)

bottom shows the Ascension as described in the Gospel According to St Luke:

> 'And it come to pass, while he blessed them, he was parted from
> them, and carried up into heaven'
> (*Luke* 24, 51)

Attention is drawn to Plate 1, where, on the title page of the *Barker* Bible (1599), the four Evangelists are depicted accompanied by an Angel, Lion, Ox, and an Eagle.

Writing on the nimbus, F. E. Hulme in *Symbolism in Christian Art* (London 1908) p 60 stated:

> 'In the fifteenth century the nimbus in the form of an equilateral
> triangle appears. It is reserved for the First Person of the Trinity
> ordinarily, though we occasionally find the dove, the emblem of the
> Holy Spirit, with a similar nimbus. As emblematic of the Trinity, it
> would manifestly be equally properly applied to any one of the three
> Persons, though ordinarily the Second Person has the circular
> nimbus, and a cross within it. In some cases beams of light radiate
> beyond the triangle, their extremities forming an exterior circle. In
> the sixteenth century, figures of the eternal Father no longer appear,
> but His name in Hebrew characters is sometimes placed within an
> equilateral triangle, and often the whole surrounded by a circular
> halo or radiation, as we see in fig. 19.'

The 'fig. 19' has been reproduced as Plate No 16, but once more we are confronted with badly drawn Hebrew.

The French author, M. Didron, in his work *Christian Iconography* (London 1851) pp 58–60 produced a most interesting example of the use of Greek letters at the extremities of the triangle as well as three sides of a cross, both appearing in nimbus form (see Plate No 17).

His comment on the drawing is:

> 'This representation of the Trinity is taken from a fresco in one of the
> Greek convents of Mount Athos. The Holy Spirit is drawn within a

16: Tetragrammaton with Triangle and irradiated Circle (16th century)

radiating aureole, the flame of which encloses within its light the two other Divine Persons. The Holy Ghost has no nimbus. The Son has a circular nimbus with the cross rays, on which are inscribed the letters The Father has a double triangular nimbus, and the three letters ὁ ὤν, are traced in the corners of that triangle, the point or apex of which is at the top.'

His general dissertation on the subject includes the following:

'In all ages, the triangle has been the geometrical emblem of the Divine Trinity. An unbroken area, terminated by three angles, expressed, with wonderful exactitude, the unity of one God in three persons. Consequently, Italy, more ideal and imaginative than France, or any other country of Western Europe, eagerly adopted for the nimbus a figure which thus symbolised the fundamental dogma of Christianity. Greece embraced the same idea, and even heightened it, declaring positively that the triangle was a fitting symbol of the Deity—of the great I AM—by inscribing, in each of the three angles, one of the letters, ὁ ὤν, THE BEING.

The Greeks, more mystical even than the Italians, were not content with one triangle only; they made the nimbus to consist of two triangles intersecting one another, and thus forming five angles instead of three. If a single triangle express the perfect divinity, two would seem to indicate the infinity of the Godhead. This idea is analogous to that of the cruciform nimbus, in which each limb further bears a cross, and is an ingenious manner of figuring the omnipotence of the Divinity.

68

It should be remarked that it has always been the practice to indicate the divine attribute by means of the nimbus. The Supreme Being is designated by the three Greek letters; the Trinity by the triangle; the infinity of God by the double triangle; eternity by the circle; life by the square, and the eternity of existence by a square within a circle.

A nimbus of triangular form, is thus seen to be the exclusive attribute of Deity, and is most frequently restricted to the Father Eternal. The other persons of the Trinity sometimes wear the triangle, but only in representations of the Trinity, and because the Father is with them. Still, even then, beside the Father, who has a triangle, the Son and the Holy Ghost are often drawn with a circular nimbus only; but in all cases these two persons of the Trinity, like the first, are alone honoured with the triangular nimbus of divinity. A copy of Dante, printed in the 16th century, and ornamented with engravings, contains, amongst others, a Trinity of three heads on one single body; this Trinity has one triangular nimbus only for the three heads.'

The *Trinity* with three heads is also to be found in the reproduction from the *Salisbury Missal* (see Plate No 14). Much of the content in M. Didron's descriptions is to be found in Freemasonry as the source material for both was similar. Considerable borrowing and adaptation has influenced the creation of mystical and symbolical devices.

17: Greek letters in Triangular Nimbus

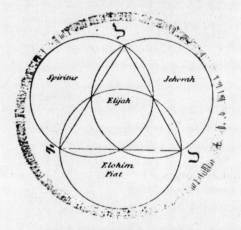

THE

USE AND ABUSE

OF

FREE-MASONRY;

A WORK of the greateſt UTILITY

TO THE

BRETHREN OF THE SOCIETY,

TO

MANKIND IN GENERAL,

AND TO THE

LADIES IN PARTICULAR.

BY CAPT. GEORGE SMITH,

Inſpeƈtor of the Royal Military Academy at Woolwich ;
Provincial Grand-maſter for the County of
Kent; and R. A.

LONDON: Printed for the AUTHOR;
And Sold by G. KEARSLEY, N° 46, Fleet-ſtreet, 1785.
[Price Five Shillings in Boards.]

18:   Title page 'The Use and Abuse of Free-Masonry' (1785)

70

The Triangles

Extensive licence has been used in placing words or characters at the extremities of the triangle. Words in Latin, English, and letters in both, as well as Greek, or Hebrew characters are to be found without difficulty and over a large range. In addition to those depicted in Plate Nos 12 & 15, it is appropriate to include another as Plate No. 16. Here, in 1785 on the title page of *The Use and Abuse of Free-Masonry*, Capt George Smith, the Provincial Grand Master and Grand Superintendent for Kent, printed a device which, amongst other elements, had Hebrew characters at the extremities of the triangle. It is an example of badly drawn Hebrew because Capt Smith apparently intended *Aleph*, *Beth* and *Lamed*, indeed it was read as such and quoted by reference to: 'Drawing of three interlacing circles with the Hebrew letters A B L and the words Spiritus, Jehovah, Elijah, Elohim, Fiat' (see p. 78, *Collected Prestonian Lectures*, 1925–1960). However the intended *Beth* is actually a *Kaph* and instead of the sound of the intended B (or V), and the appropriate application of that in combination with the other letters, the result is somewhat similar to the employment of KH or even the use of *Heth* (CH). The situation was ripe for misinterpretation and ingenious manufacture once again.

In the first Elizabethan era the triangle and the Trinitarian device even appeared in architecture. Longford Castle in Wiltshire was built as 'a comparatively large house designed in the form of a triangle, with a tower at each angle' (see Plate 19). The work was planned by John Thorpe and the building commenced in 1580, having been commissioned by Sir Thomas Gorges, a favourite of the Queen. On Cromwell's orders (c. 1660) it was, to a great extent, destroyed, but by 1678 it had been restored. W. H. Rylands quotes:

> 'On Thorpe's plan, in the middle of this triangular court is the Trinitarian device, with the word *Deus* in the middle, and *Pater*, *Filius* and *Spiritus Sanctus* in the outside corners. The outside words are connected with the central word '*est*' and with each other by '*non est*.' The device, therefore, reads *Pater est Deus*, *Filius est Deus*, etc., if taken one way, and if taken the other it reads *Filius non est Pater*, etc.'
> ('Notes on some Masonic Symbols,', *A.Q.C.* Vol. 8, p. 98)

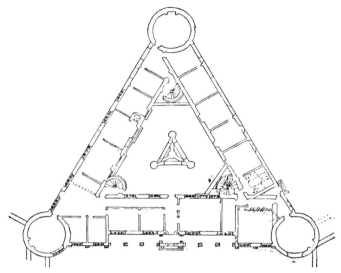

19: Plan of Longford Castle (1580)

To bring us right up to date in this subject we cannot do better than refer to the 1977 Jersey postage stamp for 1p. This bears the Trinitarian device with P (Pater), F (Filius), S (Spiritus) at the extremities of a triangle, which is more in the form of a shield, and those letters all linked with D (Deus) in the centre. The issue commemorates 'The parish of Trinity' (see Plate 20).

Soul of Nature

The name given to the triangle is said to signify 'Soul of Nature' and the basis for this is inspired from the writings of Plato, as indeed have other attitudes been so influenced. The following extracts from one work of his, *Timaeus*, will give some indication of the guidance in this:

> '. . . the maker did not make two universes or an infinite number, but
> our universe was and is and will continue to be his only creation.
> . . . in fashioning the universe he implanted reason in soul and soul in

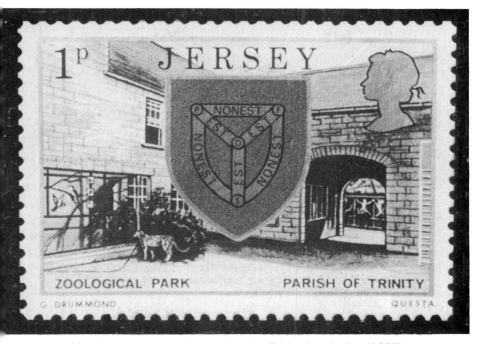

20: *Jersey postage stamp showing Trinitarian device (1977)*

body, and so ensured that his work should be by nature highest and best.

... we should think of the most authoritative part of our soul as a guardian spirit given by god, living in the summit of the body, which can properly be said to lift us from the earth towards our home in heaven; for we are creatures not of earth but of heaven, where the soul was first born ... If therefore a man's attention and effort is centred upon appetite and ambition, all his thoughts are bound to be mortal ... But a man who has given his heart to learning and true wisdom and exercised that part of himself is surely bound if he attains to truth, to have immortal and divine thoughts, and cannot fail to achieve immortality as fully as is permitted to human nature.

... Finally when the bonds of the triangles in the marrow fail and part under the stress, the bonds of the soul are also loosened; and

when this happens in the course of nature the soul departs gladly— for everything that takes place naturally is pleasant, whereas what is contrary to nature is painful. So a death by disease or injury is painful and unwelcome, but one that brings life to its natural close by old age is of all deaths least distressing and brings more pleasure than pain.'
(Translation by H. D. P. Lee, *Penguin Classics*)

We need hardly remind ourselves that Plato was born c 428 and died 348 BC and that his philosophy has had a telling influence in all periods. It is not at all surprising that it should be found in masonic writings and works.

Names for the Triangle

Only one word is to be dealt with in this study but the words to be found include the following: Abiruach; Abruach; Abroeth; Ebrioth; Abroath; Abraoth; Abrouth; Abrath; Avolet; Aberowith; Abrowith; Abberswith; Abba-with; Araboth; Ab Rabboth; Ahaboth; Abraboth; Abrohuth; Abohut. Abraxas (see Bibliography). The next section will deal with what was, in all probability, the 'parent' word.

AB RUACH—AV RUACH

Following upon the examination of the Hebrew word LAB, which has been taken to represent 'heart' and by poetical interpretation to be equivalent to 'spirit', it is proper to deal with the actual word for spirit and that is RUACH. AB RUACH is the name, in some Chapters, given to the Triangle on the pedestal. The term is formed from the following Hebrew characters:

ח	ו	ר		ב	א
HETH	VAV	RESH		BETH	ALEPH

The word AB translates as Father and has already been dealt with in this study. The second word, RUACH, has up to fifteen meanings which include 'spirit', 'breath', 'wind', so 'Father *of the* Spirit' is a legitimate translation.

Biblical References

'... and the Spirit of God moved upon the face of the waters. And God said, Let there be light: and there was light.'
(*Genesis* 1,2–3)

'And the Lord God formed man *of* the dust of the ground, and breathed into his nostrils the breath of life: and man became a living soul.'
(*Genesis* 2,7)

'And, behold, I ... do bring a flood of waters upon the earth, to destroy all flesh, wherein *is* the breath of life, from under heaven; ...'
(Genesis 6,17)

In the original the word RUACH appears where the above quotations have 'Spirit (*of God*)' and 'breath (*of life*)'. Thus there is an affinity between the expressions AB RUACH, as the name for the Triangle, and LAB BAL as one of the combinations previously dealt with; interpreted masonically as 'Father of the Spirit' and 'Spirit Lord' respectively.

THE NAMES GIVEN TO THE TRIANGLE

English Royal Arch Masons are familiar with the following phrases:

> The Egyptians termed it [i.e., the Triangle] the Sacred Number or
> Number of Perfection, and so highly was it prized by the Antients
> that it became among them an object of worship . . . They also called
> it . . . which signifies Soul of Nature.

This explanation of the triangle in the First Principal's Lecture contains
a word that has caused much confusion owing to its many and varied
forms. Two copies of the same ritual, but of different editions, can be
compared, and each will have a word that differs from the other; and
this happens in several established 'Workings'. When questioning the
use of a given word, the interested inquirer usually meets with a quite
simple explanation: 'That is the word I learned at my Chapter of
Instruction', and, for him, the matter ends there. For this reason the
word changes frequently, not only from Chapter to Chapter, but from
Principal to Principal within the same Chapter.

Lawrence F. Hemmans in his *Notes and Comments on the Royal Arch
Ritual* (Smith, London ed.):

> The word translated Soul of Nature is variously pronounced in
> different Chapters and has probably become distorted by oral
> transmission.

This is an over-simplification and fails to embrace the words that
obviously are quite differently grouped.

Why do the words vary? What is meant by Soul of Nature? Why
relate this expression to the triangle? What are we really talking about?
In pursuit of possible solutions to these questions, I have been
encouraged to collect what information is available to me and to
present this paper in the hope that perhaps it will shed light on the
subject for some Companions or prove to be a starting point for others
of student inclination or with academic leanings.

Under the heading, 'The Sacred Delta', the Rev G. Oliver wrote
(*Institutes of Masonic Jurisprudence*, Spencer, London 1859):

At the opening of a Chapter a certain word is suggested by the formation of a Sacred Delta which the present lectures explain as the '*Soul of Nature*' and '*Summum Bonum*', while in the original formula introduced by Brother Dunckerley it is thus illustrated: 'We enter the chapter on the Holy Bible with an equilateral triangle; because the scroll which was found formed a portion of that sacred book; and the equilateral triangle or delta placed thereon constitutes a striking symbol of the great reference contained in that book, *viz.*, the Trinity in Unity.'

We are at a loss to conjecture by what means or with what design the Soul of Nature was introduced into Royal Arch Masonry as a substitute for the above appropriate reference of the Sacred Delta; unless, indeed, we resort to the forced conjecture that as the name of Pythagoras occurs in ancient Masonry, in connection with the doctrine of numbers, so the modern revisers of this Order conceived themselves to be under the necessity of copying so pregnant an example by the introduction of a sage of equal celebrity, and interpreting the above expressive symbol by a reference to the far-famed *trial* and *quaternion* of Plato . . .

On page 16 of *Lectures of a Chapter, Senate and Council*, translated from the French by John Yarker (J. Hogg, London, 1882), in reply to the question:

'What signifies the triangle with its three points, the circle and the square?' [the following answer is given:]
'The triangle represents the triplicity of nature; the mineral kingdom; past, present and future; birth, life, death; body, soul, spirit. The square symbolises Nature and the four elements. The circle the eternal succession of life.'

In the same work, on page 86, when speaking of the initiates into the wisdom of Egypt, it is stated:

'The triangle, which they called the geometrical God, was the emblem of Isis and is seen traced on the Isaic table.'

Under the following headings, Albert G. Mackey has written (*Encyclopedia of Freemasonry*, 1874)

'Supports. The triangle is the Masonic symbol of God, who is, after all, the true support of the Lodge.'

'Triangle. The *equilateral triangle* appears to have been adopted by nearly all the nations of antiquity as a symbol of the Deity in some of His forms or emanations . . .'

'Tetractys. So much did the disciples of Pythagoras venerate the tetractys that it is said that they took their most solemn oaths, especially that of initiation, upon it. The exact words of the oath are given in the '*Golden Verses*' and are referred to by Jamblichus in his 'Life of Pythagoras' . . . 'I swear it by him who has transmitted into our soul the sacred tetractys, the source of nature, whose course is eternal.' Jamblichus gives a different phraseology of the oath, but with substantially the same meaning. In the symbols of Masonry, we will find the sacred delta bearing the nearest analogy to the tetractys of Pythagoreans [Fig. 1]. The outline of these points form, it will be perceived, a triangle; and if we draw short lines from point to point, we will have within this triangle nine smaller ones [Fig. 2].'

(Fig. 1)   (Fig. 2)

If we acknowledge that the equilateral triangle is represented as a symbol of the Deity, Triune or otherwise, and common to many nations and creeds, the expression 'Soul of Nature', in that context, is not therefore unfitting. According to G. D. Ginsberg (*The Essenes. The Kabbalah*, n. p. 114 (Routledge & Kegan Paul, London, 1955)) in the *Talmud* it is declared that:

'The human souls which are to be born have their abode in the seventh heaven:'
'That they leave gradually the storehouse of souls to people this earth.'

Thus, the human soul, once in fellowship with God, cannot even by death be separated from God.

The definition of Soul has divided theologians and philosophers from the earliest times. Heraclitus wrote:

> 'Though thou shouldst traverse every path, thou couldst not discover the boundaries of 'Soul'; it hath so deep a meaning.'

Therefore it would be outside the bounds of this survey to attempt such an expedition, but, for our purpose, the expression 'Soul of Nature' may be taken to imply 'Source of Life'—'The Creator'—'Father of All'.

The Ceremony of Exaltation provides a setting for the three Lectures, culminating in that given by the First Principal, the Mystical Lecture, the whole spirit of which is contained in the attempt to convey some impression of the Omnipotence, the Omniscience and the Omnipresence of the Almighty.

Contrary to what is said in the Lecture, however, none of the words that 'name' the triangle are Egyptian, nor do they originate from that source. Most of them are non-words that have sprung into being through mistranslation, mis-spelling, mispronunciation or misunderstanding perhaps of the dialect of another Companion. From whatever cause, the result is the use of many meaningless corruptions. None of the words in use can be made to translate Soul of Nature. The major proportion of the words are corruptions of one Hebrew expression—AB RUACH.

The first word, AB, is well known to all as 'Father', the B being interchangeable with a V. The second word, RUACH, may be translated as 'spirit', 'wind', 'breath'. 'Father of the Spirit' or 'Father of the Breath' would, therefore, be an acceptable translation for the whole expression. This would be in sympathy with any of the following quotations:

> 'And the Lord God formed man of the dust of the ground and breathed into his nostrils the breath of life and man became a living soul.'
> (*Genesis* 7, 2)

> 'Thou sendest forth thy spirit, they are created.' (*Psalm* 104, v 30

'Then shall the dust return to the earth as it was and the spirit shall
return unto God who gave it.'
(*Ecclesiastes* 12, 7)

—all of which truly describe the life-giving powers of the 'Father of the
Spirit' or 'Father of the Breath'—AB RUACH—'The Creator'.

It is in the translation from Hebrew characters to English letters that
the problems make an early appearance. A rudimentary knowledge of
the Hebrew language will soon make quite clear what has happened in
certain of these transformations. In the Mystical Lecture it is said of the
characters at the angles of the triangles:—

'The ALEPH, BETH and LAMED of the Hebrew correspond with
the A, B and L of the English alphabet.'

This is a misdirection, for, contrary to what is said, it must be
understood that the A in English is not equal to the Hebrew ALEPH.
The ALEPH is a consonant, not a vowel, and its use in Hebrew is
entirely different. The BETH is transliterated as B or BH; phonetically,
it may be translated as B or V, according to the manner of its
presentation. The Hebrew alphabet, being composed of 22 consonants,
has its vowels indicated by a complex system of dots and cyphers
known as 'pointing'.

As a parallel to this situation, in English, consider the cryptic
expressions one may read in the small-ad columns of some newspapers,
e.g., Rms. for rooms, Htr. for heater. Ask a foreigner to supply his own
vowels to these consonants and some very odd words would arise. This,
however, is exactly the predicament in which some ritual compilers,
revisers and printers must at times have found themselves, especially
where knowledge of Hebrew was limited. It has presented a wide field
for the development of non-words.

A full list of the 'words' collected for survey, showing the source and,
where applicable, the publisher, is embodied herewith, and reference to
this is recommended.

The two words, AB RUACH, consist of the Hebrew characters
Aleph Beth—Resh Vav Heth and are shown below, written in correct
form from right to left:

ח	ו	ר		ב	א
CH	V	R		B	A
HETH	VAV	RESH		BETH	ALEPH

The pronunciation of this expression is *Av Roo-Ach* with a guttural ending.

There is but a small difference between the two Hebrew characters *Heth* and *Tau*. The *Tau*, it will be noticed, has a small serif or foot at the base of the left leg:

ת	ח
TAU (th)	HETH (ch)

The *Heth*, in pronunciation, has the sound or power of 'ch', as in the Scottish word 'Loch'. The *Tau* is pronounced with the sound of 'th' as in the words 'Ruth' or 'myth'. Failure to read these Hebrew characters correctly, mistaking the *Heth* for a *Tau*, causes the composite word 'Ab-Ruach' to become 'Ab-Rua*th*'.

I believe that all the following 'non-words' can be traced to the ill-treated parent word, AB-RUACH:

ABRUATH	ABRATH	ABROATH	ARBROATH
ABRAOTH	ABROHUTH	ABROUTH	ABROWITH
ABEROWITH	ABBERSWITH	ABBA-WITH	ABROETH

The rituals in which these forms are used are listed in the Table of Names below.

At some time or other we have all heard the word 'Brethren' mispronounced as 'Bretheren', or the word 'Freemasonry' mispronounced as 'Freemasonery'. Such phonetic corruption could account for the word 'Aberowith' from 'Abroeth', which itself is a stray from AB RUACH.

ARBROATH has been guilty of causing confusion to those Companions who think in terms of Scottish football.

From ABRAOTH it is not a far cry to EBRIOTH. It is possible that this may have been inspired by KEBRAOTH or CABRAOTH (both borrowed from another Masonic source not very far distant).

81

ABROHUTH was produced by the compiler of the Stockport ritual in 1893. He states that it is a literal interpretation of 'Father of the Spirits', and it would therefore appear that his intention was the plural of AB RUACH. ABROHUTH approximates to the Hebrew characters which this plural form would require.

Reference has been made to the Seventh Heaven as being the 'Abode of Souls unborn', and we are not unfamiliar with the expression 'seventh heaven' as being a measure of great joy and pleasure. Plurality of heavens has, in fact, been common to several religions. The early Hebrews gave names to each of theirs, and to the seventh they gave the name ARABOTH.

Of this particular heaven, the Rev Dr A. Cohen quotes (*Everyman's Talmud*, 1932)

> 'Araboth is that in which are righteousness, judgment and charity, the storehouses of life, of peace and of blessing; the souls of the righteous, the spirits and souls which are still to be created, and the dew with which the Holy One, blessed be He, will thereafter revive the dead.'

ARABOTH, in addition to being the name of the seventh Heaven, is also the plural of ARABAH, which signifies 'Desert or Plain—an arid region'. It is clearly irrelevant to our words in the Royal Arch and the following extracts demonstrate this beyond all doubt:

> '(a) With the article, Ha-Arabah, 'The Desert', it denotes the desert tract which extends along the valley of the Jordan from the Dead Sea to the Lake of Gennesareth ... but (b) when this is not intended, and the word is used for other districts, or parts of the valley of the Jordan—as, for instance, the 'Plains of Moab' or the 'Plains of Jericho'—there the article is omitted, and the word is in the plural, ARABOTH. The two will be found in juxtaposition in II Kings, xxv, 4, 5. 'The King fled by the way toward the plain (Ha-Arabah); but the Chaldees pursued after him, and overtook him in the plains (ARABOTH) of Jericho.'
> (*Sinai and Palestine*, p 487, The Rev. A. P. Stanley, 1871)

There is no indication that I can find regarding the choice of this word to describe the triangle, but it should be noted that ARABOTH is an anagram of ABROATH. This does pose the question: 'Has there been an attempt here to solve a mystery where only accident created one?'

With some similarity in writing and in sound to ARABOTH is the expression AB RABBOTH, which could only signify 'Father of Many' and cannot be equated with 'Soul of Nature'. It has made an appearance merged into one word, ABRABOTH. Speculation in this field by Lawrence F. Hemmans produced the word AHABOTH, which, he states, signifies 'Desires'.

Another group of words consists of:

AVOLET   AVOLETH   AVOULOUTH   ABOLETH

According to one writer (Stockport ritual), 'the word AVOLET is composed of the letters at the angles of the triangle, *viz*, A, B and L, together with one branch of the Triple Tau, a T'. This is taking into consideration the interchangeability of the letters B and V. In one manuscript that I inspected in Grand Lodge Library, BH is shown written above the letter V, and, in another, TH written above the letter T. The word ABOLETH would, therefore, be written in Hebrew as shown here:

ת	ל	ב	א
TAU	LAMED	BETH	ALEPH
T or Th	L	B or V	A

The word could thus be interpreted as AVOLET, AVOLETH, ABOLET or ABOLETH. The last one has made an appearance elsewhere as the latter part of the word MANABOLETH. This is used in the tract, dated 1724, entitled 'A letter from the Grand Mistress of the Female Freemasons to Mr Harding the Printer (*History of the Grand Lodge of Ireland*, Lepper & Crossle, 1925). In this tract, various maimed and mock Hebrew words are referred to in the following manner:

'This play with the Hebrew alphabet is very antiently call'd the *Manaboleth*.

In a later part of the tract the process is changed and is then described:

'They made a kind of *Manaboleth* in English.'

The use of the word, in this context, infers that nonsense has been employed in order to confuse or obscure. The Hebrew word for 'foolishness' (EE-VEL-ETH) could be stretched into anglicised form to AVOLET.

Shepherd-Jones has written (*Ten Talks on the Holy Royal Arch*)

'The antients call the triangle A ... B ... H signifying the "Soul of Nature". The old word *Abraxas* is not now used in our ritual.'

Whilst I have not seen a ritual that uses this word, it has received the attention of Masonic writers—Wellins Calcott in 1769 and William Hutchinson in 1775.

Of this word the *Encyclopaedia Britannica* states:

'Abraxas or Abrasax. A word probably first used by the Basilidians and engraved on certain antique stones called on that account Abraxas stones. The letters in the Greek notation make up the number 365, and the Basilidians gave the name to the 365 orders of spirits which emanated in succession from the supreme being. These orders were supposed to occupy 365 heavens, each fashioned like but inferior to that above it, the lowest being the abode of the spirits who formed the earth and its inhabitants to whom was committed the administration of its affairs. In addition to the word Abraxas, the stones often have cabbalistic figures engraved on them.'

Sir E. A. Wallis Budge wrote (*Egyptian Magic*, 1901)

'On papyri and amulets the (Greek) vowels are written in such a manner as to form triangles and other shapes; with them are often found the names of the seven archangels of God' ... 'but of all the names found upon Gnostic gems, two, i.e., Khnoubis (or Khnoumis) and Abrasax (or Abraxas) are of the most frequent occurrence.'

'Considerable difference of opinion exists as to the meaning and derivation of the name Abrasax, but there is no doubt that the God

who bore it was a form of Sun-god and that he was intended to represent some aspect of the Creator of the World.'
(*ibid.*, p. 180)

Again, speaking of the 'Magic' Papyrus (British Museum, 10,042):

'It is quite certain that the Gnostics and other sects which held views akin to theirs obtained the names which they were so fond of inscribing upon their amulets from this source.'
(*ibid*, p. 175)

ABHT, ABHAHUTH, AV HUTH—I am informed—are the anglicised forms of the Aramaic and Syriac word for 'Fatherhood'. ABOTH is the Hebrew word for 'Fathers' or 'Patriarchs', and ABAHATHA is another Semitic word for 'Patriarchs'. The words ABOHUT and ABOHOT, in Royal Arch usage, must be transcriptions from ALEPH BETH HE TAU, and the intention, I feel, here was to convey the principle of 'Fatherhood'. This would be in keeping with the reference to 'Father of all'—the first stanza of Alexander Pope's *Universal Prayer*, which has been introduced into the triangle portion of the Mystical Lecture.

Some rituals have dots in place of a word for the triangle, whilst others have an initial letter followed by dots, or part of a word with dots indicating omission of letters. Those with dots only are really in the 'do-it-yourself' class, thus permitting Companions complete freedom of choice. Those with letters and blank spaces tend to create added confusion; an example of this is A . . . r . . . h having been interpreted as ARAUNAH!

In the Table of Variants, I have shown where, in a stated ritual, the word has changed from one form in one edition to something else in a later publication. Nowhere can I ascertain the reason, nor yet the authority for such a change; such things are not recorded, and the publishers, where I have applied, cannot assist.

Recognising that although a word is meaningless or unintelligible to us, that does not necessarily make it so, also that mystery names were long ago chosen with great care in order to obscure an idea from the uninstructed, I have made this survey within the scope available to myself and set out the result at 'layman' level in order that the many will see the subject in true perspective. The expert will have already examined it for himself and arrived at his own conclusions. To have attempted to discuss the Hebrew words using vowel signs *in extenso* would have taken the subject beyond the point of interest for the majority, but I am fully aware that much ground can still be covered at a Masonic Hebrew 'graduate' level. It seems pointless to me to dismiss the subject of the word for the triangle as being elementary and trivial when, for 100 years and more, the words, however maimed or distorted, have served a purpose of sorts.

In conclusion, I submit that the naming of the triangle was an introduction into the ritual, to amplify the 'Oneness' of the Creator; that it was related to the triangle merely to bring a 'Creator'-explanation that would add to the Trinitarian explanation; that the statement, 'The Egyptians called it . . .', etc., was introduced to lend the situation an air of antiquity. The term that was used, being Hebrew, produced its own contradiction, because, being so little understood, it has been subjected to revision, amendment, alteration and 'improvement' at the hands of subsequent revisers. It was an importation to the ritual around the mid-nineteenth century, but, contrary to what has been said on many occasions, it *cannot be established* that the Rev George Adam Browne was responsible for it.

Should the 1834–35 situation recur, *viz*, an official revision or reshaping of the Royal Arch Ritual, then the 'naming' of the triangle portion of the Mystical Lecture is an item that should, justifiably, come under review.

TABLE OF VARIANTS

Name	Source	Publisher	Date
Av Ruach	Sussex Ritual	Lewis, London	3rd Edn., 1958
Abiruach	Manuscript GL 16,348	—	—
Abiruach	Ritual booklet	Private	Undated
Abruach	'The Mystical Lecture' Perram (GL No BE395/5 PER.)	Typescript	—
Abroeth	Sussex Ritual	Lewis, London	1st Edn., 1932
	Sussex Ritual	Lewis, London	2nd Edn., 1946
	Perfect Ritual	Lewis, London	1926 *et seq.*
	Metropolitan Ritual	Lewis, London	1884, 1897, 1917
	Metropolitan Ritual	Lewis, London	1938, 1963
	Complete Ritual	Lewis, London	1921, 1941
	Taylor's Ritual	Taylor, London	3rd & 4th Edn.
	Universal Ritual	Toye, London	—
Ebrioth	Grenadiers' Ritual (as taught in C. of I.) Holmes-Dallimore	Reeves, London	—
	Cornwallis Ritual (in use of C. of I.)	Kenning, London	Revised Edn.
	Castle Ritual (by Northumbrian P.Z.s)	Smith, Newcastle	1924
Abroath	Metropolitan Ritual (as worked in C. of I.) Manuscript GL 15,153	—	—
	Metropolitan Ritual	Kenning, London	3rd Edn.
	Metropolitan Ritual (printed for C. of I.)	Straker, London	—
Abraoth	Andrews' Ritual (GL 268)	Andrews, London	1893
Abrouth	Manuscript GL 15,159	—	Undated
Abrath	Underhill Ritual	Underhill, Plymouth	1921
	The Sections of the H.R.A. Degree from a manuscript hitherto unpublished (GL 15,121)	Westcott, Plymouth	—

Name	Source	Publisher	Date
AVOLET	*Ceremony of Exaltation*	Bradshaw, London	1851
	Text Book of Freemasonry	Reeves & Turner	1874
	Text Book of Advanced Free-		
	masonry	Reeves, London	1873
	Claret Ritual	Private, London	1866, 1873
	Northumbrian Ritual	Smith, Newcastle	
	(GL 15,136)	Privately printed	1889
AVOLET &			
ABEROWITH	Oxford Ritual	Lewis, London	1884 *et seq.*
ABROWITH	Manuscript GL 15,159	—	—
ABBERSWITH	Ritual, GL 16,080	Privately printed	—
ABBA-WITH	Manuscript (book)		
	Reg No 19324/116	M.M. Hall Library	—
ARABOTH	Aldersgate Ritual (Nigerian)	Lewis, London	1957, 1960
AB RABBOTH	*The Exaltation Ceremony*		
	GL 15,690	—	—
	Manuscript GL 15,132	—	—
AB RABBOTH	*Notes and Comments on R.A.*		
& AHABOTH	*Ritual,* Hemmans	Smith, London	—
ABRABOTH	*L'Arche Royale de Jerusalem*	Frederick Printing	
		Co.	—
ABROHUTH	Stockport Ritual (compiled		
	for Charity Chapter, No		
	323)	M.M. Hall	
	Reg No 19328/1116	Swain, Stockport	1893
ABOHUT	Perfect Ritual	Lewis, London	1874, 1st Edn.
			1877 *et seq.* to 192
	Domatic Ritual (as taught by		
	C. of I.)	Pobjoy, London	1960
	Domatic Working Ritual	Toye, Kenning &	
		Spencer, London	1961 Edn.
	Croneen Ritual (GL 16,682)	Privately printed	1905
A.B.O.H.U.T.	Hornsey (Sections)	Keening, London	1929
ABOHOT	Humber Ritual (Chapter No		
	57)	Private, Hull	1930
ABRAXAS	*Historical Analysis of the*		
	H.R.A. Ritual, Castells	Lewis, London	1929
	Ten Talks on the H.R. Arch,		
	Shepherd Jones, GL 10,148	Private	—

Table of Variants

Name	Source	Publisher	Date
A	Aldersgate Ritual	Lewis, London	1921, 1948
A .,	Hornsey Ritual	Kenning, London	1941, 4th Edn.
A . . . r . . . . H	Complete Ritual	Lewis, London	1892 to 1920
	Midland Ritual	Privately printed, Birmingham	1918
	Also—(Revised by a Committee of Representatives of the Provinces of Warwick, Worcester and Stafford, and Approved by the G.Sup. of the Provinces)	—	1926, 1929
	Taylor's Ritual	Taylor, London	1904, 1st Edn.
AB . . . . B . . . H	Aldersgate Ritual (Nigerian)	Lewis, London	1946
. . . . (Only dots are shown)	Standard Ritual (in use in the C. of I.)	Privately printed	1920
	Standard Ritual	Kenning, London	1960 Edn.

ROYAL ARCH RITUALS

In which the Word has been Changed in Different Editions

PERFECT	Lewis, London—1874 *et seq.* until 1926	ABOHUT
	Lewis, London—1926 *et seq.* .	. ABROETH
COMPLETE	Lewis, London—1892 *et seq.* until 1921	A . . . . r . . . . h
	Lewis, London—1921 *et seq.* .	. ABROETH
METROPOLITAN	Lewis, London—1884 . . .	. ABROETH
	Straker, London (undated) . .	. ABROATH
	(As practised since 1866 in C. of I.)	
SUSSEX	Lewis, London—1932 (1st Edn.) .	. ABROETH
	Lewis, London—1958 (3rd Edn.) .	. AV RUACH
TAYLOR'S	Taylor, London—1904 (1st Edn.).	. A . . . . r . . . . h
	Taylor, London—1904 (4th Edn.)	. ABROETH
NORTHUMBRIAN		
CASTLE RITUAL	Smith, Newcastle—1889 . .	. AVOLET
	Smith, Newcastle—1924 . .	. EBRIOTH
ALDERSGATE	Lewis, London—1944 . . .	. AB . . . B . . . H
	Lewis, London—1957 . . .	. ARABOTH

CONCLUSION

Because its emergence and development was not uniform throughout this or any other country we have no clear view of the founding of Speculative Freemasonry. Among the influences in the growth was the patronage bestowed by those who commissioned work from the operative stonemasons, and the intelligentsia who were consulted from time to time on such projects. Perhaps the strongest influence came from members of Trade Gilds in the main cities.

In like manner we are denied reasons for the adoption of the various legends that made their appearances, some to fade away and others to remain. We have only shadowy and sparse references to guide us in those early writings. The possiblity is that the portrayal of the medieval 'Mystery Plays' by the various Trade Gilds, in different parts of the country, inspired the introduction of some of the action. Nearly all those Plays had a morality lesson and a biblical theme in which it was imparted; in effect they were extensions of the church and became yet another reason for Assembly in the Saxon and Norman periods when the church was the centrepiece of life in general.

Owing to the chameleon-like qualities of Freemasonry, much of what was perfectly clear to the 'fathers and promoters' became somewhat clouded for many of their successors. Alterations, sundry graftings and accretions, so-called improvements, even occasional pruning, who can say how far away is the practice of today from whatever it was at the beginning? Each amendment may well have been made with good intention but it is more than probable that sometimes it was effected by an ill informed improver, or one who was determined to alter its course for future generations. Notwithstanding the efforts of the protagonists for universality, each age has produced its own experts, its own idealists who have been allowed to tamper or improve according to opinion; never changing the whole but constantly whittling away or adding to *what was*, trying to shape *what should be*.

It is no small wonder that some senior members who are unable to devote the time necessary to analyse some of the more complex issues contained in the foregoing, now find themselves in the same state as a first year student on being handed a fourth year text book. The unravelling of the many intricate windings tend to confirm the Freemasonry has been no one main project throughout its history, but the development of many branches from the large number of roots it has put down, starting in the medieval era and maintaining a growth that has been unabated. It displays its adaptability to cater for all men and shows itself as a true 'Center of Union, and the Means of conciliating true Friendship among Persons that must have remain'd at a perpetual Distance' as it was so well described in the *Antient Charges*. ('Concerning God and Religion'—1723 *Constitutions*)

GUIDE TO PRONUNCIATION

Yielding to many requests the author has compiled the following list to convey a common pronunciation of the Anglicised forms of non-English names or words that occur in Royal Arch masonry. No attempt has been made to cater for native or localised dialect. With regard to Hebrew, the different sects will adhere to their own pronunciations, but so far as Latin is concerned, as the true pronunciation has been lost, there are separate schools, literally, in the treatment of that language. If a particular form is preferred then that surely is the one to use for one should be true to the truth that one knows. What is 'right' to one Companion may be 'wrong' to another and the purists should be left to argue among themselves, as well as the rival schools. Speaking of 'Rivals', Sheridan's effort in particular, this guide may well be of assistance to a Companion who perhaps through lack of acquaintance with a given word or expression may otherwise have trodden in the footsteps of Mrs Malaprop; who has not heard an inclusion of that nature in Freemasonry?

In some words the letters 'I' and 'J' are interchangeable, as indeed are 'J' and 'Y', and often the letters 'B' and 'V' in Hebrew. An example of this kind of adaptability is shown in the word 'Alleluia' which occurs in Revelations, chapter 19, and may be seen printed as 'Halleluiah' or 'Halleluyah', or 'Hallelujah'. It derives from the Hebrew 'Hallal' for 'praise' and 'Jah' which is an abbreviated form of the Ineffable Name to mean LORD and occurs in *Psalm* 68. It is often used as a suffix in Hebrew names amongst which are: Eli*jah*, Isa*iah*, Josi*ah*, Jeremi*ah*, Nehemi*ah*, and Zedek*iah*, which all have an obvious meaning that refers to God.

Where stress should be voiced the phonetic spelling in this list has the appropriate syllable underlined.

Aaron	*Air*-ron	Adoniram	Ad-don-*iram*
Abiathar	*Ab*-i-*ay*-thar	Ahasuerus	Ah-*has*-u-*air*-ous
Abif or Abiv	Ab-*if* or Ab-*iv*	Ahiman	*Ah*-he-man
Abinadab	*Abbin*-a-dab	Ahimelech	Ah-*he-mel*-leck
Abraham	*Ay*-bra-ham	Ahiram	Ah-*hi*-ram
Acacia	Ac-*kay*-sha	Ahitub	Ah-*he*-toob
Adonai	Ad-don-*eye*	Aholiab	A-*ho*-le-ab

Aleph	*Al*-ef
Alleluia	Al-le-*lu*-yah
Amalekites	Am-*mal*-e-kites
Ammi	*Ar*-mee
Amorites	*Am*-mor-rites
Araunah	Ar-*rawn*-nah
Artaxerxes	Ar-tax-*erk*-seas
Babel	*Bay*-bel
Babylon	*Bab*-e-lon
Benedicat	Ben-ne-*de*-cart
Benedictus	Ben-ne-*dic*-tous
Benedicto	Ben-ne-*dic*-tow
Benedicatur	Ben-ne-*de-car*-tour
Berith	Be-*rith* or Ber*it*
Bethlehemite	Beth-le-*hem*-mite
Bezaleel	*Bez*-ar-leel
Boaz	*Bo*-az
Brethren	*Breth*-ren
(not 'Brether-	
en' please)	
Chaldean	Kal-de-an
Cherubim	Cher-roo-*bim*
Cyrus	*Sy*-russ
Darius	Da-*ri*-uss
Dodecahedron	Do-*decca*-he-dron
Ecclesiastes	Ecc-*clee*-se-*astees*
Eleazar	*El*-le-*ay*-zar
Eliab	E-*li*-ab
Eliel	E-*li*-el
Elohe	*El*-o-ee or El-o-*hay*
Ephraim	E-*fray*-im
Exaltation	Ex-alt-*tay*-shun
Ezekiel	Ez-*zeek*-eel
Gedaliah	Ged-a-*ly*-yah
Giblites	*Gib*-lites
Giblim	*Gib*-lim
Hagar	*Hay*-gar
Haggai	*Hag*-eye
Halidom	*Hal*-e-dom
Harodim	*Harro*-deem
Horeb	*Hor*-reb

Icosahedron	I-*cos*-a-*he*-dron
Isaiah	I-*zi*-yah
Ishmeel	*Ish*-may-el
Israel	Is-*ray*-el
Issachar	*Iss*-a-kar
Jachin	*Jar*-kin
Jebusite	Jeb-u-*zite*
Jehoachin	Je-*ho*-a-kin
Jehosaphat	Je-*hos*-a-fat
Jeremiah	Jerry-*my*-yah
Jerusalem	Jer-*ru*-sar-lem
Josedech	Jo-se-*deck*
Josiah	Jo-*si*-yah
Jubelo	Ju-be-*low*
Japhet	*Jay*-fet
Judea	Ju-*dear*
Kodes	Ko-*desh*
Kebraoth	Ke-*bray*-oth
Kadosh	Kad-*dosh*
Lamed	*Lar*-med
Machabon	*Mark*-ha-bon
Machabonai	*Mark*-ha-*bone*-eye
Machbenah	*Mark*-ben-ah
Magen	*May*-jen
Mahalaleel	Mah-*ha*-la-*le-el*
Maher	*Mar*-her
Mannasseh	Man-*nass*-er
Mattaniah	*Matt*-an-*i*-yah
Melchizedech	Mel-*kiz*-ze-deck
Melech	*Mel*-leck
Menatschin	Men-*at*-skin
Moriah	Mor-*ri*-yah
Naamah	Nay-*ah*-mah
Naphtali	Naf-*ta*-lee
Nathan	*Nay*-than
Nebuchadnez-zar	Neb-bu-kad-*nezzar*
Nebuzaradan	Neb-bu-*zarra*-dan
Neder	*Nee*-der
Nehemiah	Nay-he-*mi*-yah
Nineveh	*Nin*-ne-vah

Noachidae	No-*ack*-e-day	Shaddai	*Shad*-eye
Noachite	*No*-ack-kite	Shalom	Shal-*om*
Noah	*No*-ar	Shealtiel	*She*-al-*te*-el
		Shiloh	*She*-low
Omega	O-*me*-ga	Sinai	*Sign*-eye
		Sojourner	*Soj*-journ-ner
Patriarch	*Pay*-tre-ark		
Potipherah	Pot-*tif*-fer-rah	Tabor	*Tay*-bor
Pythagoras	Py-*thag*-gor-as	Tabernacle	*Tabber*-nackle
		Tau	Taw
Rabboni	*Rab*-bon-eye	Thummim	*Thum*-im
Ramah	*Ram*-ah	Tirshatha	Ter-*shar*-tha
Raphael	*Raf*-fay-el		
Reuben	*Ru*-ben	Vespasian	Ves-*pays*-ze-an
Ruach	Ru-*ark*		
Ruhamah	Ru-*ar*-mah	Zadok	*Zay*-dock
		Zebulon	*Zeb*-u-lon
Sacerdotal	*Sas*-ser-*doe*-tal	Zechariah	Zeck-ar-*ri*-yah
Salem	*Sar*-lem	Zedekiah	Zed-e-*ki*-yah
Samaria	Sam-*air*-ree-ah	Zeredatha	Zer-*red*-a-tha
Sanhedrin	San-*hed*-rin	Zerubbabel	Zer-*rub*-ab-bel
Seraphim	*Serra*-fim		

A detail from the Kirkwall Scroll (18th century)

The exact date of the Kirkwall Scroll is not known but it is attributed to the third quarter of the 18th century. It is 18ft 6 inches long and 5ft 6 inches wide, painted on strong linen which consists of a full width of cloth in the centre with a divided width sewn along each side for its full length. The items featured on it are crudely painted, mainly in pale blue, and on each side of the central strip is a ribbon of three colours, blue, yellow and green. The centre is divided into sections, the top representing the Creation and the garden of Eden with Adam, animals, birds, and fishes. The border on the left is intended to represent the wanderings of Abraham and his eventual arrival in Egypt. That on the right, reading upwards, has a road marking a total of 44 years and commences with the Exodus from Egypt with detail of events until reaching the Promised Land. The sections marked off on the centre panel, below the first panel for the Creation, shows various Christian symbols as well as emblems of several degrees of freemasonry; each succeeding section has additional symbols of both. This Scroll is in possession of Kirkwall Kilwinning Lodge in Scotland.

21: The Kirkwall Scroll

BIBLIOGRAPHY

The source for each quotation or extract used in this study has been shown at the appropriate point in the text. Many Papers on subjects allied to those covered have been read but have not required reference therein. They are to be found in the published *Transactions* of the various Lodges of Research throughout the world. Prominent among the writers are the Rev C. J. Ball, Rev Morris Rosenbaum, Rev Canon W. W. Covey-Crump, and Rev H. Poole.

Extracts from the French publications have been taken from the English translations collated in *Early French Exposure, 1737-1751,* edited by Bro Harry Carr and published by Quatuor Coronati Lodge in 1971.

The *Barker* and other Bibles in the libraries of QC Lodge and the United Grand Lodge of England have been used in this work and the author wishes to record his appreciation of the facilities made available in the period of research by Bro T. O. Haunch, Librarian and Curator, Freemasons' Hall, London.

Finally, a constant companion throughout this exercise has been Dr Robert Young's *Analytical Concordance of the Holy Bible* (8th Edn. Lutterworth Press), a scholarly work first published in 1879. In his Preface the author trusted that his readers might 'give themselves more to the study of the ORIGINAL Scriptures, which have God for their Author, Truth without mixture of Error for their Matter, and Salvation for their End.'